THE PROPHETS AND THE LAW

JOSEPH RHYMER

THE PROPHETS AND THE LAW

SHEED AND WARD

FIRST PUBLISHED 1964
SHEED AND WARD LTD
33 MAIDEN LANE
LONDON W.C.2

NIHIL OBSTAT: JOANNES M. T. BARTON, S.T.D., L.S.S.
CENSOR DEPUTATUS

IMPRIMATUR ✠ PATRITIUS CASEY, VIC. GEN.

WESTMONASTERII, DIE 28 AUG. 1964

The *Nihil obstat* and *Imprimatur* are a declaration that a book or pamphlet is considered to be free from doctrinal or moral error. It is not implied that those who have granted the *Nihil obstat* and *Imprimatur* agree with the contents, opinions or statements expressed.

This book is set in 11 pt. Linotype Times

Made and printed in Great Britain by
William Clowes and Sons, Limited, London and Beccles

To my parents

CONTENTS

INTRODUCTION

Anyone who sets out to write about the Old
Testament should be aware of his limitations. I
should like to make it clear at the beginning that
I do not think of myself as writing with any kind
of particular authority. I am very far from knowing all there is to know about the Old Testament,
or even the small part of it which is discussed in
these pages. My only claim is that of a student
who perhaps has had more opportunity to study
the Old Testament than some others have had,
and I hope that some may be encouraged to study
it by what I have written. If a subject is worth
giving time to it will open out and expand as
the student quarries into it, and he will dis-
cover whole areas and aspects whose existence
he had never suspected. This is certainly true of
the Old Testament, but it is not easy country to
explore and this book will have served its purpose
even if it only provides an opening, a point of
entry, by which the exploration may be begun.

I hope no-one will be tempted to try to get by
without reading the parts of the Old Testament
covered in these pages. Difficult though they may
be, the Prophets' own books are the best place to
learn about their experience of God and his

saving work; reading them makes the difference between the man who only knows a country from looking at a map and the man who has trodden the ground himself. It helps, of course, if we read it in a translation which is not too far from our everyday language; with this in mind the quotations are all from the Revised Standard Version, a recent translation which is faithful to what the Old-Testament authors actually wrote and at the same time does not sound strange to modern ears. I have used the names of people and of books of the Old Testament in the form given by the Revised Standard Version. There are only two places where these may be unfamiliar to some readers: the two books of Paralipomena are called 1 and 2 Chronicles, and the four books of Kings are called 1 and 2 Samuel and 1 and 2 Kings. Where a reader might be confused the other form is given in brackets after the reference. The Revised Standard Version can be obtained in paperback at a very moderate price.

It only remains to thank the theological students and the West Indian audience who listened patiently to much of what is in this book, and who by their comments and questions helped to make it clearer.

JOSEPH RHYMER
Moor Park School, Ludlow

"And I will walk among you, and will be your God, and you shall be my people."

Lev. 26.12.*

1

THE GROUND

No matter at what stage we happen to be in our studies there is one great danger for all of us, and that is of forgetting that the Old Testament is about people who lived and loved and had jobs and families and joys and anxieties, just as we have. The Old Testament is a book which has had an enormous influence. This is so obvious that one feels a little foolish pointing it out. At the merely political level it has been appealed to by all sides, absolute monarchists right through to republicans, as a guide to the relations between men in society: king and commons, citizen and foreigner, master and servant—even owner and slave. The ancient Hebrew customs can be used and misused as guides—and have been. At the cultural level its influence has been felt all through the Western world, particularly since the sixteenth century, when the upsurge of the Renaissance brought with it the modern translations of the Bible into the ordinary language of the people. Since then, particularly, much of the very way that the Hebrew people thought has become our way of thinking, just as many of their turns of speech have found their way into modern English. And I need say nothing of their influence in the sphere of religion; two of the most influential living faiths both have their roots in the religion of the Old Testament: Christianity and the Moslem faith.

It is in the very extent of this influence that the danger lies for us when, in the twentieth century, we examine the Old Testament. It is easy for us to think we already know all about it, or at any rate all that is important about it. And even when we are prepared to admit to ourselves that much of the Old Testament is dark and obscure to us, we still think that there is something shameful about admitting this. It is not that familiarity has bred contempt, but rather, ironically, that familiarity here breeds ignorance. There are two initial steps we can take which will help us avoid these dangers. The first is to go back to the text itself. But here there is a difficulty: this is not one book, but thirty-nine books, and moreover, books referring not to just one period in the history of a people but to centuries of change and development and growth. I hope I may have helped solve this difficulty by the choice I have made of this particular period in the history of the Hebrew people: the two hundred years from Amos's preaching until the Babylonians captured and destroyed Jerusalem. For it is during this time that the earliest of the books was written, and the writings of this period are easy to see against the historical background and also give the key to understanding a great deal of the rest of the Old Testament.

The other step is to try and remember all the time that these are people. I have already hinted that we may run into difficulties if we forget that the Old Testament is a number of books; in the same way we shall never get near to it if we forget that it was written by people and for people, and that they were people influenced by the history and thought of their own times even when they were themselves helping to create that history and thought. The *first* questions we must ask when reading any book of the Old Testament are: What is the setting of this book? What did the writer *mean* when he wrote it, and what did his readers make of it then? We must try and get into the skins of the people of the time, and think with their minds and feel with their hearts. The best word for this is "sympathy"; we must try to be sympathetic towards these people and enter into their experiences. It is only when we do this honestly that their experiences begin to throw light on our own situation. But we must first forget our own situation so that we can enter as fully as possible into theirs.

What, then, were these people like? What kind of forces and influences were they exposed to?

In many ways the pattern of experience for these people was made for them by their geographical position. To the north and north-east of Palestine there lies the great fertile river basin of the land of Euphrates and Tigris, Mesopotamia, as it was called, the Land between the Rivers. In a straight line between Mesopotamia and Palestine there is nothing but desert, country which may support scraggy sheep with difficulty if you keep them moving as they finish off what little grass there is, but not country you go into if you can help it, and certainly not country which would support an army on the move. But there is a good route north out of Palestine through Damascus and Hamath and Haran, and then the whole of Mesopotamia lies open, stretching away to the south-east.

To the south lies Egypt, the broad and muddy delta where the River Nile runs into the Mediterranean, and then the thin ribbon of highly fertile country on either bank of the river for hundreds of miles into Africa. The river was the nation's life blood, bringing fertility from the desert, and her only road, and because the Egyptians depended so much on it, the river easily became their god as well, source of life and prosperity.

Between these two great cradles of civilization lay Palestine, a narrow belt of fertile country. Her position made her the natural corridor between Mesopotamia and Egypt. When there was peace between the two great civilizations the Hebrews also had peace—and profited from the merchants who trod the road that ran along the coast and up to Damascus and across into Assyria or Babylon. When there was war that same road carried armies living by what they could take and strong enough to crush any opposition so small a people as the Hebrews might be able to offer. Then their only hope was to buy off the invader and pray that they pass through quickly, or drive the cattle into the small walled towns and abandon the crop and pray that the invader would not bother to spend time on a siege. It is easy to see why Palestine has been called the cockpit of the Middle East—and also why so many cultures met and blended there and left their mark on the people of the land.

Whichever of the neighbouring Great Powers happened to be strong tried to control the Hebrews' country and make it their first line of defence against invasion. And always the Hebrews were tempted to turn to one or other of the Great Powers for help and protection—a situation not unknown nowadays. But there was this difference, and a big one too: nowadays the great powers are often only too glad of the opportunity of establishing bases, and they will pour in money and supplies to help develop the country. But the Hebrews paid for the support of Assyria or Egypt with gifts and the risk of occupation if the gift was not large enough. Begging the support of one of the Great Powers meant for the farmer and merchant and householder heavier taxes and perhaps the expense and anxiety of supporting foreign troops in the country. And not only that. Alliances were naturally sealed by the exchange of gods. An alliance with Assyria meant that the Assyrians expected the Hebrews to add the Assyrian gods to their own worship and find place in the Temple for Assyrian altars and Assyrian statues. In an age when there was no division between politics and religion the nation's worship must reflect the political situation. Little wonder, then, that the Prophets were so anxious for the country to keep clear of these alliances. Hosea was typical of all the Prophets when he wrote:

> Ephraim is like a dove,
>> silly and without sense,
>> calling to Egypt, going to Assyria.[1]

Then, speaking in the name of God, he continued:

> Woe to them, for they have strayed from me!
>> Destruction to them, for they have rebelled
>>> against me!
> I would redeem them,
>> but they speak lies against me.[2]

[1] Hos. 7.11.
[2] Hos. 7.13.

Yet one cannot help but feel for these people, lying like corn between the upper and lower millstones, in danger of being crushed whenever Egypt or Assyria moved.

Only once in her whole history was the nation free from this anxiety, and that was a time when neither Mesopotamia nor Egypt was powerful enough to be able to put any pressure on Palestine. By about 1150 B.C. the power of Egypt had spent itself, and civil war weakened her further so that not for 400 years was she a power to be reckoned with. At the same time the old Babylonian empire in Mesopotamia was swept away by barbarian hordes which flooded down from the mountains behind her. She was to be replaced indeed, and replaced by the most terrifyingly cruel power in the ancient world, Assyria, but again 350 years were to pass before the pressure of the rising power of Assyria was felt by the Hebrews.

It was during these 300 years of freedom from outside pressure that the Hebrew kingdom was born and reached its flowering in the reigns of David and Solomon. The memory of that glory went deep into the hearts of the people and every boy's ambition was to be a second David and restore his country's greatness again. The man who had been king and poet, shepherd and outlaw, victor over the Philistines and maker of peace and unity between the tribes of his own people captured the imagination of the people and never lost it again. When the unity and freedom had gone and the people began to look to God to deliver them again with a high hand and an outstretched arm, they had David as their model, they asked him to send them another David. Isaiah wrote of the coming saviour-king whose name would be called

Wonderful Counsellor, Mighty God,
Everlasting Father, Prince of Peace.[1]

But he went on to say that it was the throne of David that he would establish again and uphold. And in the dark days just before the fall of Jerusalem and its destruction, Jeremiah wrote:

Behold, the days are coming, says the Lord, when I will raise up for David a righteous Branch, and he shall reign as king and deal wisely, and shall execute justice and righteousness in the land.[2]

But the kings who followed David were not of his stature, not even his son Solomon, and when Solomon died the brief political and religious unity collapsed and the nation divided into two kingdoms. It need not surprise us very much. The cleavage came along the lines of strong enough tensions between the northern and

[1] Isa. 9.6.
[2] Jer. 23.5f.

southern parts of David's kingdom. There were differences in customs, and particularly a difference of a month between the times of crop for the two parts of the country. This meant that the dates of the feasts which everyone was expected to attend at Jerusalem were inconvenient for the northerners. The strong central administration which Solomon had built up at Jerusalem had made it easy for him to tax and control and organize the country, and the people had deeply resented his interference.

The breach was never healed and Assyria was only too swift to exploit and widen it, for it made her control of the area easier. Just when our period starts, as Amos was preaching in the northern kingdom, Assyria gathered herself together under King Tiglath-Pileser III and set about making an empire for herself. From that moment onwards the threat of Assyria hung heavy over the whole country. In great sweeping campaigns, rumours of which would penetrate into every Hebrew farm and city, Tiglath-Pileser secured his rear in Mesopotamia and marched west and south towards Palestine. He had found a new way of crushing any nationalism in the people he conquered; he uprooted them and scattered them in small groups throughout his empire, so that they could never again unite against him.

We have an echo of the fear the Assyrians in-
spired. Nahum describes an Assyrian army on the
move:

> The shield of his mighty men is red,
>   his soldiers are clothed in scarlet.
> The chariots flash like flame
>   when mustered in array;
>   the chargers prance.
> The chariots rage in the streets,
>   they rush to and fro through the squares
> they gleam like torches,
>   they dart like lightning.[1]

> The crack of whip, and rumble of wheel,
>   galloping horse and bounding chariot!
> Horsemen charging,
>   flashing sword and glittering spear,
> hosts of slain,
>   heaps of corpses,
>   there is no end of corpses,
>   they stumble over the corpses.[2]

If you or I had lived in the path of Assyria that
picture would never have been far from our
minds. At first we should have learned it from the
refugees flooding down the road from the north
and telling what they saw in their district before
they escaped. The great alabaster plaques have
been discovered which Tiglath-Pileser had carved

[1] Nahum 2.3ff.
[2] Nahum 3.2f.

to commemorate his victories; they show besieged cities in flames and prisoners impaled outside the walls. Soon there would be no need of the tales of refugees and travellers, for the northern kingdom, Israel, tried to defy Assyria and was crushed. In 721 B.C., just when Isaiah had started to prophesy in the southern kingdom of Judah, her neighbour, Israel, was destroyed and her people scattered, never to be heard of again. Only a few years later the folk in Jerusalem itself watched from the city walls an Assyrian army camped round them, and heard the Assyrian general appeal to them to surrender and save themselves the horrors of a siege. Nothing they could have done could have saved them, but some kind of pestilence swept through the Assyrian ranks and so decimated them that the army had to return to Assyria. Once there the king was assassinated, and no later Assyrian king again mounted an attack on Judah. She was to be spared for the attention of the next great Mesopotamian empire, the Babylonian, which broke Assyria and Egypt, deported the people of Judah and destroyed Jerusalem.

But the struggle for political independence and freedom was not the only problem, or the most important one for this people, at this time. Equally urgent was the struggle to purify the people's idea of God and his worship. This was the outstanding work of the prophets whose books we shall be

examining in the rest of this book. What beliefs
did those prophets find in the people among
whom they lived? What beliefs had they themselves been taught in the country village of Amos,
the small city of Hosea, the Jerusalem of Isaiah
or the priestly family of Jeremiah?

We must remember that at this time there was
no Bible in anything like our sense of the word.
Even the first five books of the Bible did not reach
their present form for another four hundred years.
But the heart of the matter was already there, the
story of the escape from Egypt and the crossing of
the Red Sea and the making of the covenant with
God at a holy mountain on the way from Egypt
to Palestine. In these events the Hebrews saw the
hand of God at work, and by these events they
believed that God had chosen them to be his
people and had shown them his power. The
proof of it all lay in the stark fact that their
fathers had been brought safely out from the
slavery of Egypt in the face of Pharaoh's army.
It is not our task here to examine how far we
may accept the biblical account of this as histori-
cally accurate in the way we now expect historical
writing to be accurate; we are only concerned to
see what ordinary folk believed at the time of
Amos and Isaiah and Jeremiah. But it is worth
noting in passing that each of the main traditions
have the Exodus, the escape from Egypt, at their
centre, and that the descriptions bear the marks

of actual events which deeply impressed those who saw them, such as the sight of powerful and feared enemies washed up dead on the beach.

But whatever happened, the people worshipped a God who had intervened decisively at a critical point in the nation's history and saved it, and who would intervene again whenever it might be necessary.

For above all their God was dependable. He had promised them that he would be their God and they would be his people, and he would keep his promise. Hosea was the one who first realized how true this is, that God's patience and dependability are proof even against his people's disobedience; but even before Hosea God's steadfast protection was very much taken for granted by the ordinary Hebrew. The story of his mighty saving acts had been handed down faithfully from father to son, and had been told again and again at the sanctuaries to which the people travelled to make their sacrifices. At least three times every year all who could travel went to sacrifice, at the beginning of the barley harvest, and at the wheat harvest, and at the end of the year when all the crops were in. During the eight days of the feast while they were living near the sanctuary, they would hear again the stories they already knew so well, and in their sacrifices would feel they were renewing their contact with this God who was so much more powerful than the Egyptian gods, and entering again into the sphere of his power. In the course of years of telling the traditions had become more and more fixed, and about this time they were being written down for the first time. But few people could read, or indeed needed to, and still the main way the traditions would be learned and remembered would be the old way of the storyteller, telling again the stories of the saving acts of their God, which most of his hearers already knew by heart anyway.

The only trouble was that when that revelation had first been given the people were shepherds, and it was only natural that they should think of their God as a shepherd God. They commemorated him at first with a typically shepherd's sacrifice, a lamb, and saw no need for any other kind of feast. It was not until they reached Palestine, and learned from the people already living there the techniques of an agricultural economy, that they felt the need for other feasts, feasts which would bring their God's blessing on each harvest as the different crops were gathered in during the year. And here was a complication, for the people who were already living in the land, the Canaanites, had gods of their own, and they wondered whether it might be wiser and safer if the sacrifices were made to those gods, for it might be that the harvests were under the control of the Canaanite gods and not of the God who had brought the Hebrews safely out of Egypt.

For long the people saw nothing wrong in worshipping other gods—provided Yahweh, their own special God, was given pride of place in their worship and at their feasts. The realization that Yahweh was not only the supreme God among gods, but more than that, grew very slowly among the ordinary people. In fact it is very probable that it was not fully realized and accepted that he alone is God until after they had passed through the furnace of the exile in Babylon and the destruction of Jerusalem.

There can be no doubt that it was the greatness of Moses' achievement to at least plant the seeds of this realization in the hearts of the people. He it was who interpreted the events of the escape from Egypt as the work of Yahweh, who gave the people the God's-eye view of what was happening to them. It is not that Yahweh wins a battle against all the other gods, and particularly the Egyptian gods; rather it is that they fade into insignificance when Yahweh shows himself as all-powerful and free to do to his own people—and other people—what he thinks is right. Strictly speaking this is not full monotheism—rather it might best be called practical monotheism—but once it was established and accepted the way was open for full monotheism to develop from it.

That development was a long time coming. Solomon himself encouraged the worship of other gods in Jerusalem and built temples for them.

And however friendly and comparatively harmless the small gods of the village shrines may have been, with influence only over the village fields, they were fertile ground in which more objectionable forms of worship could take root and grow. In particular they became centres for the worship of the mother-goddess Astarte, the giver of fertility; and the local *baals*, or lords, who gave fertility to the village fields, became Astarte's husbands. The worship was accompanied by sexual licence and sacred prostitution. In the end the Hebrews were bound to reject all this if Yahweh meant anything at all to them, and in the end, of course they did reject it, but it took a long time. After Moses had laid the foundation in 1223 BC his work was continued by the great line of teaching and writing prophets whom we shall be considering, men who lived five hundred years after Moses.

But more important, perhaps, even than the work of the Prophets, was the achievement of a man or small group of men whose name or names we do not know. During the spiritually dreary years of Manasseh's reign, when the northern kingdom of Israel had died and when Isaiah's work in the southern kingdom of Judah was finished, these men made the first great collection and codification of the nation's laws. But more than that: it was more than a mere collection of laws and traditions. They took the insight into

the character of God which had been Moses'
gift to the nation he created; and they took the
deepening of that insight which had been given
to Amos and Hosea and Isaiah; and they applied
this knowledge of God to every detail of the daily
lives of the people, showing them how it ought to
find expression in all they said or did, and in
the way they treated their fellow citizens. The
result of their work is the Book of Deuteronomy.
Deuteronomy stands at the centre of this period
we are examining as its summary and essence,
and the peak of its achievement.

If we examine the *immediate* results of the
Deuteronomists' work, if we look at the *short-*
term effects of the impact of Deuteronomy on this
people, then there is only one verdict possible: It
failed. At first it impressed itself on king and
people by its vision of the omnipotence and love
of God, of the fatherhood of Yahweh: caring for
his people, and grieving over them, as a father
for a beloved son. Josiah the King initiated a great
reform which was to purge the nation of all that
was unworthy of their position of honour as the
chosen of God and his favourite children. Idols
were destroyed and the pagan places of sacrifice
desecrated; the priesthood was reformed and
sacrifice forbidden at the local village shrines
where so much of the pagan influence and fertility
practices were centred. Jerusalem and the Temple
were made the source of the religion of the whole

people, the only place of sacrifice, the central sanctuary to which all adult males in the whole country must go for the great feasts. If one were to look for a slogan for Josiah's reform, then "One God, One Altar" would serve. One God, one altar, one people united and purified in his worship and service.

It was a noble vision and a noble attempt. But it failed. About this time the great Assyrian Empire collapsed and Nineveh itself fell to the rising power of the Babylonians. Egypt tried to snatch the opportunity of regaining her former glory and power; Pharaoh Neco marched north at the head of an army and in a forlorn and hopeless gesture Josiah marched out to oppose his passage. The two armies met at Megiddo in the Valley of Jezreel, where the coast road passes under Mount Carmel and strikes inland for Damascus and the north. Josiah's servants carried him, mortally wounded, back to Jerusalem to die, and with him died the reform. Ten years later the Babylonians captured Jerusalem for the first time, and ten more years after that they destroyed it.

To those twenty years of approaching catastrophe belong Jeremiah's ministry and the terrible vocation of preaching hope in an apparently hopeless situation. But he it was who alone saw through the approaching catastrophe into a future when a purged and purified chosen remnant of the people would return with new hearts and a new covenant to be the centre of God's salvation of the world.

Only on the shortest of views can it be said that the work of the men who wrote Deuteronomy failed. Look only a little further and their achievement is monumental. Even if others from Moses onwards had laid the foundations and hewn out the stones, it was the authors of Deuteronomy who built the structure of Hebraic monotheism, and that structure was going to stand. It was they who saw the history of the Hebrew people through God's eyes, and communicated this vision to the people. The Book of Deuteronomy itself is the start of it, and probably the greatest literary factor in it, but the whole sweep of the nation's history, from the entry into Palestine right through to the fall of Jerusalem, is given in the great series of history books which is the work of the Deuteronomists: the books of Joshua, Judges, 1 and 2 Samuel and 1 and 2 Kings (1, 2, 3 and 4 Kings). With them the Bible as we now know it began to take shape.

Let me end this chapter as I started. We must remember that these are people, not just vague figures dressed in peculiar clothes and living a hopelessly long time ago. These are people and we must try to get inside their skins if we are to appreciate their achievement. This is not easy, but it is essential if we are to understand these people and respect their greatness.

AMOS

AMOS is the first of the line of prophets who left behind them a report of their teaching in written form. He lived about the year 750 BC, and it is significant that it was about this time that the main traditions of the nation, centred on the escape from Egypt and the Covenant with God at the Holy Mountain somewhere between Egypt and Palestine, first appeared in written form. Until then they had been passed on by word of mouth from father to son and priest to priest, but now the written word began to come into common use, and the traditions were finally fixed as documents. Before Amos we are dependent on later tradition; with Amos for the first time we have a written report made very near to the time when he was teaching. For this reason alone we can now move with confidence when we examine his teaching; we do not have to depend on the report of someone living much later—with all the dangers of colouring the report with a picture of his own times rather than the times of Amos.

This is important, because the history of this

time was all written by a later historian who was far from writing history as we think of writing history. The man who wrote the two books of Kings, which are our main source for all the political history of this time, was mainly concerned with showing the importance of the Temple at Jerusalem and its services. To be sure, he had in front of him the official court diaries and records of the two states of Israel and Judah, but he only copied from them, on the whole, the dates of the kings, and anything about the Temple and the religion centred round it; he decided whether a king was good or bad largely by whether he supported the Temple or ignored it and its priests. In all fairness to him, we must remember that he didn't set out to do much more, and if there is something interesting he has left out he tells us to go and look it up for ourselves. Again and again the tantalizing words occur: "And the rest of the acts of Joram [or Ahaziah, or Jehu, or whoever it might be], are they not written in the Book of the Chronicles of the Kings of Israel?" Well, they might have been at one time but they have long been lost to history, for one thing is certain: the book he speaks about isn't the Book of Chronicles (Paralipomena) we have in our Bible now.

When Solomon died nearly two hundred years earlier, the precarious unity David had created collapsed. David was one of those rare men of

2

dynamic personality who could attract loyalty and maintain it in the face of the strongest of pressures and tensions. Even so, there were some tense moments in his life when his throne and the country's unity were within an inch of collapse. Solomon his son held the peace mainly through commercial success, great personal prudence (on which his later reputation for wisdom is based), and a gift for magnificent display. Surely one of the most attractive descriptions in the Old Testament is the one reporting the Queen of Sheba's reactions to the magnificence of Solomon's court:

> And when the queen of Sheba had seen all the wisdom of Solomon, the house that he had built, the food of his table, the seating of his officials, and the attendance of his servants, their clothing, his cupbearers, and his burnt offerings which he offered at the house of the Lord, there was no more spirit in her.[1]

We musn't go into too much detail about what happened at his death, or we shall never get to Amos. It must be sufficient to say that his son Rehoboam, led on by the young men of his own age, tried to steamroller his way to kingly power without the tact and concessions which alone could back that power with loyalty. The northern and most powerful part of the kingdom revolted. Ready to lead them was the man whom Solomon

[1] 1 Kings 10.4f. (3 Kings 10.4f.)

had put in charge of all the labour employed in the extension and fortification of Jerusalem, and this man, Jeroboam, they took and crowned. Rehoboam assembled an army to crush the northern insolence and restore the unity of his throne, but the army refused to march against men who had so recently been their brethren, and the chance was lost. From now on there was a growing hostility between the two kingdoms, Israel in the north, and Judah (centred on David's capital, Jerusalem, and the Temple) in the south. The subsequent history is one of border incidents and small battles, and of periods when the two came to an uneasy agreement for a year or two and then broke up again. It is against this background of nearly two hundred years of rivalry and suspicion and treachery and occasional battles between the two kingdoms that Amos is placed, somewhere around the year 750 BC. His task was an explosive one. A citizen of the southern kingdom of Judah, his unenviable vocation was to travel into the hostile northern neighbour, Israel, and denounce it at one of the leading religious centres. It says much for his courage that he carried out his mission; he was lucky to escape with his life.

Amos lived in the small country village of Tekoa, in the heart of the most barren part of the highlands of Judah overlooking the Dead Sea. Bethlehem is about two hours' walk away.

About all that can profitably be raised in that part are sheep and goats. Amos was one of the local shepherds, and a shepherd, moreover, not of the fat plains sheep raised for their meat, but of the hardy and wiry mountain sheep raised for their wool. His writing breathes at every point the sharp uncompromising spirit of the hardy mountain shepherd, familiar with discomfort and danger in the care and protection of his flock. Country comparisons and figures of speech abound. He warned the people that God's anger could crush them as the sheaves of corn stacked at the bottom of a harvest cart are crushed[1]; if they hoped for rescue from God's wrath it could be no more than like pickings left by a lion after the flock has been attacked:

> As the shepherd rescues from the mouth of the lion two legs, or a piece of an ear . . .[2]

There is not even safety in flight in the face of a lion, for there are other dangers in this wild stretch of country:

> As if a man fled from a lion and a bear met him; or went into the house and leaned with his hand against the wall and a serpent bit him.[3]

But in any case we are not dependent on such scraps of internal evidence in his writing, for he

[1] Amos 2.13.
[2] Amos 3.12.
[3] Amos 5.19.

says plainly that he is no professional prophet
trained in one of the prophetic schools attached
to some local sanctuary:

> I am no prophet, nor a prophet's son; but I
> am a shepherd, and a tender of sycamore trees:
> and the Lord took me from following the flock,
> and the Lord said to me, Go, prophesy to my
> people Israel.[1]

Those words were Amos's reply to the chief
priest of the Israeli royal sanctuary of Bethel,
where Amos went to preach. When Jeroboam I
accepted the crown from the northern tribes there
was much to be done before his new kingdom
could be secure. Not least he had to make sure
that his people's loyalty was no passing whim.
His greatest danger lay in the religious traditions
and esteem which surrounded Jerusalem. When
David made it his capital he moved the Ark
there, the most sacred religious object in the land,
which some said contained the tablets on which
the Law was carved, and others said was the
earthly throne of God. For long the people had
been used to journeying to Jerusalem at the
greater festivals, and Solomon had secured its
religious importance by building the Temple to
house the sacred Ark. If the people of the new
northern kingdom of Israel still went on religious
pilgrimages to the Temple in the heart of the

[1] Amos 7.14f.

capital of Judah it would not be long before they again looked on it as their political capital, and Jeroboam's control of his kingdom would be ended.

He solved the problem by taking the two most ancient and important of the local sanctuaries of the northern kingdom, Bethel in the south on the road to Jerusalem, and Dan in the far north, and making them royal shrines. With its own official religion and its own official royal sanctuaries Israel hoped to keep the loyalty of its people and wean them away from any loyalty towards Judah. It was to the nearest of these two shrines, Bethel, that Amos made his way in response to God's call.

His prophetic mission was not an easy one. He had crossed into comparatively hostile country and he was to speak in a royal sanctuary where any criticism was only too likely to be interpreted as treason. He could not even appeal to any officially recognized prophetic standing if he was challenged. He went about it, in a very clever way, by shooting first at targets which would arouse the approval of the crowd:

Thus says the Lord:
For three transgressions of Damascus, and for
    four, I will not revoke the punishment . . .
For three transgressions of Gaza, and for four,
    I will not revoke the punishment. . . .[1]

[1] Amos 1.3,6,9 etc.

He first attacked Israel's immediate enemies: Damascus, capital of Syria; Gaza, centre of the Philistines; Tyre, capital of Phoenicia; Edom, below the Dead Sea; Ammon and Moab to the east. In each case the introductory formula means: "It is no use pleading that only three or four wrongs have been done, each has been involved in unnumbered crimes, and must be punished."

The crimes listed by Amos give an interesting and chilling insight into the dangers to which folk were exposed in the everyday life of a small and not very powerful country. The troops of Damascus, just north of Israel and once part of David's kingdom, had driven their iron-wheeled chariots over prisoners of war. The Philistines of Gaza had rounded up whole districts and sold them into slavery; the Phoenicians of Tyre had driven their slave trade across a treaty of friendship with Israel. Edom to the south, closely related to the Israelites, had ruthlessly attacked her despite all ties of kinship—the Edomite "corrupted his compassions" says the Hebrew, most expressively. The Ammonites had hideously mutilated pregnant women and the Moabites had committed sacrilege by desecrating the corpses of their enemies. No wonder the Israelites listened to Amos with approval as he predicted the vengeance God would bring upon all these nations.

But better still, Amos the Judaean next attacked Judah itself:

Thus says the Lord: for three transgressions of Judah, and for four, I will not revoke the punishment . . .

but he did not specify Judah's crimes, he only said generally that they had rejected the law of the Lord. And finally, as some of the listening Israelites must by now have expected, he turned on Israel. He had reached his point at last.

But there was more to this approach of Amos's than a mere clever technique which would gain him a hearing. He was saying something important about the extent of God's power and the claims he made over peoples other than Hebrews. At this time it is doubtful whether the ordinary Hebrew man in the street, the man who went regularly to the sacrifices at the local sanctuary, thought that God, *his* God, Yahweh, had any power outside Hebrew territory. We get a glimpse of this attitude in Naaman, the Syrian general, who came down from Damascus to see if Elisha could cure him of his leprosy. Elisha did cure him and Naaman wished to remain under the protection of this powerful God, Yahweh, whom Elisha worshipped. And this is the significant thing: in order to be able to worship Yahweh when he was no longer in Hebrew territory. Naaman asked if he might take away with him some of the *soil* of Israel:

Then Naaman said, ... Let there be given to
your servant two mules' burden of earth; for
henceforth your servant will not offer burnt
offering or sacrifice to any god but the Lord.[1]

No ordinary Israelite of the time would think his
request strange, and Elisha did not stop him.
Within Israel and Judah Yahweh their God was
supreme, there was no doubt about that, and
Elijah had demonstrated it conclusively in his
victory over the official prophets of Baal, but an
Israelite travelling *outside* his own country at that
time would not have been quite so sure about
Yahweh's power to protect him then.

Amos showed not only that the God of the
Hebrews cared about other people, but more than
that, that he held them responsible for their
actions and would punish them for their crimes.
This is a decisive step, and a long one, along the
road which ends with the full recognition that
there is only one God and that he is omnipotent,
omnipresent and omniscient. The full realization
of this will not come until after the period of exile
in Babylon, a full 250 years after Amos, but the
heart of the matter is already there. Let the people
of Damascus and Gaza and Tyre and Edom and
Ammon and Moab take care, for the Hebrew God
is concerned with their affairs too.

Amos had reached the point in his preaching
which he had travelled so far to make. It needs

[1] 2 Kings 5.17. (4 Kings 5.17.)

little imagination to visualize the silence as the people realized he was going to speak about *them* now, the dying away of the murmurs of approval. Amos brought to bear on the everyday life of Israel his shepherd's vision of a powerful and uncompromisingly righteous God. His description of everyday life in the northern kingdom is not a very pretty one:

Thus says the Lord:
For three transgressions of Israel,
    and for four, I will not revoke the punish-
        ment;
because they sell the righteous for silver,
    and the needy for a pair of shoes—
they that trample the head of the poor into the
        dust of the earth,
and turn aside the way of the afflicted;
    a man and his father go in to the same
        maiden,
    so that my holy name is profaned;
they lay themselves down beside every altar
    upon garments taken in pledge;
and in the house of their God they drink
    the wine of those who have been fined.[1]

And I raised up some of your sons for prophets,
    and some of your young men for Nazirites . . .
But you made the Nazirites drink wine,
    and commanded the prophets,
    saying, You shall not prophesy.[2]

[1] Amos 2.6ff.
[2] Amos 2.11ff.

He returned to some of these charges later, and in particular to the injustice committed against the poor, and the contemptuous treatment of them by the rich and those responsible for the administration of justice. He connected all this with the luxury and prosperity brought in by the long years of peace. For although there had been internal friction between Israel and Judah, this had been a period free from any interference from the great empires to north and south. Although Assyria was poised and ready she had not yet swept down into Palestine, and Israel and Judah's merchants had done well from the trade passing through the country. The great houses they had built only help to bring into sharper relief the poverty and injustice in which many of the people lived:

> I will smite the winter house with the summer
>   house;
>   and the houses of ivory shall perish,
>   and the great houses shall come to an end,
>   says the Lord.
> Hear this word, you cows of Bashan,
>   who are in the mountain of Samaria,
> who oppress the poor, who crush the needy,
>   who say to their husbands,
>   Bring, that we may drink![1]

But not only are they left in physical need, and made to pay a disproportionate amount of the

[1] Amos 3.15f.

country's taxes: "You trample upon the poor, and take exactions from him of wheat." Worse than this was the corruption of justice. The magistrates used to meet and hold court in the market place just inside the city gate, the most public place in the town and the one place all had to pass through when entering or leaving it. But now, says Amos, the city gate only sees bribery and the poor man always losing his case:

> For I know how many are your transgressions,
>   and how great are your sins—
> you who afflict the righteous, who take a bribe,
>   and turn aside the needy in the gate.[1]

And yet all this went on while the round of services and sacrifices was maintained in the sanctuary; more than that, even, one of the ways of robbing people was to lend them money on security and then dedicate for Temple use the property deposited as security. This meant that the borrower could not get his property back even if he could repay the loan. So the injustice was carried into the Temple services and the very worship of God corrupted by it.

Here again, Amos was breaking new ground, or at any rate ground new to the ordinary Hebrew, in his insistence that mere regularity and faithfulness in worship is not enough, God also requires of his people righteousness in their

[1] Amos 5.12.

dealings with one another. To us this is commonplace and obvious. That it is so is the most impressive testimony to the success of the teaching of Amos and those who came after him. It is not easy for us to think our way back into the thoughts of an ordinary Hebrew worshipper of Amos's day; let one example be enough. There is a Hebrew word which means "to set apart", "to consecrate". Everything associated with the worship of God is something set apart, something consecrated. From this same Hebrew word comes the word for "holy". Anything consecrated is holy. The priest is holy because he is dedicated to the service of God. The Temple and all its fittings are holy because they are set apart for God's worship. It comes as a shock to us to find that the Temple prostitutes were also called "holy", and not merely at some very primitive early period in Hebrew history, but at this time and right on up to the fall of Jerusalem to the Babylonians. They are referred to four times in the Books of Kings alone at various periods from Rehoboam's reign immediately after the death of Solomon through to King Josiah's reform only thirty years before the monarchy was destroyed by Babylon along with Jerusalem.[1] At this time "holiness" carried with it no moral consequences. It was not yet realized that holiness

[1] 1 Kings 14.24; 15.12; 22.47. 2 Kings 23.7. (3 Kings and 4 Kings.)

must be accompanied by righteousness; that anyone set apart for the service of God must also be virtuous, honest, upright. The failure to realize this was, of course, a failure to realize what God is like. In all this criticism of their everyday life Amos was revealing to them his insight into the character of God.

So this is the other important thing that Amos had to say about the character of God. He was not only a God whose power stretched beyond the confines of Israel and Judah. He was also a righteous and just God, who required that his people should not only be faithful to him and regular in their worship, but also lead moral lives and be just in their dealings with one another. He had chosen this people, and protected them, and it was his power which had brought them safely out of the degradation of slavery in Egypt: more than that, it was the same power which created and controls the world:

> For lo, he who forms the mountains, and
> creates the wind,
> and declares to man what is his thought;
> who makes the morning darkness,
> and treads on the heights of the earth—
> the Lord, the God of hosts, is his name![1]

But this power was not exercised in an arbitrary way; God used it to declare and protect his own integrity, his righteousness, his own purity, and he

[1] Amos 4.13.

did so by punishing any who tried to take advantage of God's favour and protection and at the same time do things of which he would disapprove.

So Amos's harshest condemnations were reserved for those people who thought they were being faithful to God in all their formal religious observances, but did not see that it need make any difference in their everyday lives. With heavy sarcasm he says:

Come to Bethel [that is the sanctuary where Amos is preaching] and transgress; to Gilgal [another sanctuary just north of Bethel], and multiply transgression; and bring your sacrifices every morning, and your tithes every three days; and offer a sacrifice of thanksgiving of that which is leavened, and proclaim freewill offerings and publish them: for this you love to do, O people of Israel, says the Lord God.[1]

Without the foundation of a moral life, or at least the attempt to live a moral life, worship is hollow and imperfect. Worse, in fact; it is sacrilege, for it implies that God tolerates or even approves the worshipper's immorality.

The first essential is to seek God as he in fact is, seek him in his righteousness and try to take that righteousness into secular life:

Seek the Lord and live; lest he break out like fire in the house of Joseph [Joseph is the tradi-

[1] Amos 4.4f.

tional ancestor of the northern people], and it devour, with none to quench it for Bethel: O you who turn justice to wormwood, and cast down righteousness to the earth![1]

Seek good and not evil, that you may live: and so the Lord, the God of hosts, shall be with you, as you have said. Hate evil, and love good, and establish justice in the gate: it may be that the Lord, the God of hosts, will be gracious to the remnant of Joseph.[2]

Amos clinched his teaching by telling these people of the visions or insights or spiritual experiences, by which God made all this known to him. There are five of them, the first three of which are tied together as a series.[3]

The first[4] is of a plague of locusts, the insect scourge which breeds at a phenomenal rate and then swarms and strips every green thing in its path. In this case it struck at the people in particular; the first crop of the year the King always took to support the army, and the people then used the second crop for themselves. But this year the locusts destroyed the second crop. At first this looked as if it was the beginning of the final destruction which God had threatened. This Amos knew would only be just and deserved, but

[1] Amos 5.6f.
[2] Amos 5.14f.
[3] Amos 7.1–9; 8.1–2; 9.1–4.
[4] Amos 7.1–3.

he pleads for another chance for these people who are his country's enemies, and God hears his plea.

The second[1] is a fire, and again the destruction stops short of wiping out the kingdom.

But the third vision[2] is of a plumbline, the simple ball of lead attached to a piece of string used by builders for testing whether a wall is standing upright or leaning to one side. There is no cheating possible with a plumbline, no getting round its decision. Either the wall is upright or it isn't, there are no two ways about it:

> Then the Lord said, Behold I am setting a plumbline in the midst of my people Israel; I will never again pass by them; the high places of Isaac shall be made desolate, and the sanctuaries of Israel shall be laid waste; and I will rise against the house of Jeroboam with the sword.[3]

There can be no compromise with the standards of God's righteousness—this is the heart of Amos's message—and the hand of God will reach anywhere that his righteousness is being ignored.

> But let justice roll down like waters,
>   and righteousness like an ever-lasting stream.[4]

[1] Amos 7.4–6.
[2] Amos 7.7–9.
[3] Amos 7.8b–9.
[4] Amos 5.24.

The other two visions only serve to drive this
further home: A basket of fruit on the very point
of going rotten; this is what Israel is like. Out-
wardly it seems good and sound, but probe only
a little below the surface and you find corruption. There is a pun in the Hebrew on the word
for "summer fruit" and the word for "end", which
sound alike:

> And he said, Amos, what do you see? And I
> said, A basket of summer fruit. Then the Lord
> said to me, The end has come upon my people
> Israel.[1]

The same point is made by the last vision, the
vision of God himself standing in the temple at
Bethel and shaking the roof onto the heads of
the worshippers:[2]

> Though they dig into hell, from there shall my
> hand take them; though they climb up to
> heaven, from there will I bring them down.
> Though they hide themselves on the top of
> Carmel, from there I will search out and take
> them; and though they hide from my sight at
> the bottom of the sea, there I will command the
> serpent, and it shall bite them. And though they
> go into captivity before their enemies, there I
> will command the sword, and it shall slay them:

[1] Amos 8.2.
[2] Amos 9.1–4.

and I will set my eyes upon them for evil, and not for good . . .[1]

Behold the eyes of the Lord God are upon the sinful kingdom, and I will destroy it from off the face of the earth.[2]

That destruction was not to come for another thirty years, and before that happened there was another prophet preaching in Israel, Hosea, whose teaching about God gave depth and tenderness to the stark and oversimplified picture Amos had drawn. But the destruction, when it did come, was complete. Assyria swept over the northern kingdom and it never again emerged.

Considering how outspoken Amos was, and that he was speaking in the royal sanctuary of the established religion, he was treated very gently by the authorities. The priest of Bethel sent to the king to ask him what to do about Amos and the treason he was speaking:

The land is not able to bear all his words. For thus Amos has said, Jeroboam shall die by the sword, and Israel must go into exile away from his land.[3]

But all he did to Amos was to tell him to go back home to Judah and prophesy there:

[1] Amos 9.2–4.
[2] Amos 9.8.
[3] Amos 7.10b–11.

Go, flee away to the land of Judah, and eat bread there and prophesy there: but never again prophesy at Bethel: for it is the king's sanctuary, and it is a royal house.[1]

But Amos told him that because he had tried to stop him speaking God's mind he would be caught up in the coming disaster and his children killed and his wife violated and he himself die in captivity.

Yet not all that Amos said was dark and hopeless. There is a note of opportunity about his teaching, even if it is a last opportunity. There is still opportunity to seek the Lord, still time to hate evil and love the good, "and establish justice in the gate: it may be that the Lord, the God of hosts, will be gracious to the remnant of Joseph."[2] As in all the Prophets, there is an element of mercy as well as justice in the character of the God Amos reveals. It is not very conspicuous, but it is there. And this is why I personally am prepared to say that the last few verses of the last chapter are in fact by Amos, and not, as some scholars hold, a later addition. Those last verses foresee a future time when the people, purged and brought to their senses, and united by a king like David, are raised into God's favour again and live in a blissfully peaceful land of plenty:

[1] Amos 7.12–13.
[2] Amos 5.15.

In that day will I raise up the tabernacle of David that is fallen, and repair its breaches, and raise up its ruins, and rebuild it as in the days of old.

Behold, the days are coming, says the Lord, when the ploughman shall overtake the reaper and the treader of grapes him that sows the seed; the mountains shall drip sweet wine, and all the hills shall flow with it. I will restore the fortunes of my people Israel, and they shall rebuild the ruined cities and inhabit them; they shall plant vineyards and drink their wine, and they shall make gardens and eat their fruit. I will plant them upon their land, and they shall never again be plucked up out of the land which I have given them, says the Lord your God.[1]

NOTE: KEY TEXTS IN AMOS

7.14–15	His prophetic call
2.13; 3.12; 5.19; 7.14	Country idioms
	Denunciations:
1.3–2.3	of surrounding nations
2.4–5	of Judah
2.6–7 and throughout	of Israel
1 Kings 11	Political background
2 Kings 14	

[1] Amos 9.11–14.

2.6–7; 3.15; 5.12; 8.4–6	Social sins condemned
2.7–8; 4.4	Religious sins
All of ch. 6	Luxury
4.6–13; 5.8–9; 9.7–10	God's power
5.6–7,14–15; 7.1–9; 8.1–7; 9.1–6	God's righteousness
9.8,11–15	God's mercy

These references are not meant to be complete, only to give some of the main points and some of the places where they are to be found.

HOSEA

THE first impression one gets from reading the book of the prophet Hosea (and I am sure your experience will have been the same as mine in this) is one of confusion. Particularly is this so after the clear-cut, black-and-white character of Amos and his teaching, for whom the issue was luminously clear and certain. From the hard and uncompromising background of the Judaean mountains Amos had discovered that God is righteous, and the realization had so deeply impressed him that he could see little else. God is righteous and those who serve him and claim his protection must also be righteous or perish. It was as simple and sure as a mason testing the wall he had built. Either it is upright or it isn't, and his plumbline will tell him. If it isn't upright it must be pulled down.

So clear was this to Amos that one feels the depth of his disappointment when the people did not listen to him, and a softer, more gentle Amos is shown to us in his lament for the unheeding northern kingdom. One glimpses a flash of tenderness in the Amos who can see these people in their original unspoiled purity, a purity which God would restore to them if they would let him do so:

> Hear this word which I take up over you in
>   lamentation, O house of Israel.
> Fallen, no more to rise,
>   is the virgin Israel;
> forsaken on her land,
>   with none to raise her up.[1]

Only a few years after Amos had left the northern kingdom of Israel to return to his native Judah with mixed feelings of sorrow and anger, Hosea appeared on the scene. But he came as a native Israelite, not as a Judaean who had crossed the hostile frontier between the two Hebrew kingdoms. These were his own people in a way that Amos could not know. For all Amos's awareness that they were one people with one God and one history, nevertheless the one people had been split into two mutually antagonistic and suspicious kingdoms for nearly two hundred years by Amos's time, and this was bound to affect deeply both his approach and his reception by the people. Hosea was involved with these people to a depth that Amos could never be, and perhaps this is why one gets the impression with Amos that he is a spectator of their tragedy rather than a participant in it.

[1] Amos 5.1f.

Again let me emphasize that our task is not to judge these people and their prophets, but to try and share their experiences. Not to assess their influence on later generations, our own included, but to appreciate their impact on their own generation. To look at their times through their eyes and, if possible, with their feelings about them. In a word, to be sympathetic.

If one approaches Hosea in this way I believe it is easy to understand why his book is confused. To be sure, there have been later hands at work editing it, men who lived after the kingdom in which Hosea lived had disappeared from history and who tried to write the moral into his teaching with their historical hindsight, and in particular men from the southern kingdom of Judah who, two hundred years after Hosea, had returned from the exile in Babylon and could see more clearly how the history was working out. Yet even when all allowance has been made for this, much confusion remains, and the cause of it lies in Hosea himself and his situation. He was involved. That is certainly part of the reason. These were his own people, and the agony he could see coming, which he could read inevitably in the external political and military forces which were beginning to focus on his kingdom, this agony was going to be as much his as anyone's. He could not stand dispassionately and watch it all develop, for he was himself in the path of the storm.

But there is a deeper reason for the confusion and contradiction in his teaching, and that confusion lies deep in the experience Hosea had in his marriage. By all the traditions and customs and laws of his time and place his marriage should have broken up. But despite the fiercest possible strains on it, it didn't do so. It was in analysing the reason for this that Hosea penetrated further into the character of God and his attitude to his people than anyone before him. We need not be surprised if he is not as clear about it all as we should like him to be. Let me repeat, we must put ourselves squarely into his situation if we are to understand what he is trying to say.

Even the *way* in which the story of Hosea's marriage is told is confusing, for it is told as if Hosea knew from the beginning that his wife was an adulteress:

> And the Lord said to me, Go again, love a woman who is beloved of a friend and is an adulteress . . .
> So I bought her for fifteen pieces of silver, and a homer and a half homer of barley: and I said to her, You must dwell as mine many days; you shall not play the harlot, or belong to another man; so will I also be to you.[1]

It *may* be that he did deliberately marry a woman whom he knew to be unfaithful already, but it is more likely that this is being told in the light of his

[1] Hos. 3.1–3.

later experience with her. It is like a man who
buys a house which turns out to be full of dry
rot, and he says, "I bought a dud there." He
doesn't mean that he knew the house was rotten
when he bought it, but that he found later that he
had wasted his money. So I believe Hosea's
experience, and his penetration into the character
of God through that experience, is best under-
stood if we see his marriage starting off normally.
Nor need we be startled by his paying a price for
her; the most reasonable explanation of this is
that it is her dowry[1]; the price, or goods, paid to
her family to compensate them for the loss of her
services, or even paid to the woman herself, for
about this time it was becoming customary for the
woman to receive the dowry her husband paid.[2]
And this question of a dowry is important for the
use Hosea made of it when he came to interpret all
this in terms of God's treatment of his people.

The marriage, then, started normally and his
wife, Gomer, bore him three children, a son, a
daughter and a son; and here we come to another
peculiarity which to our eyes is difficult to understand: the names Hosea gave his children. The
first boy he called Jezreel; and his daughter he
called Lo-runamah, which means, "That has not
obtained mercy"; and the other boy he called
Lo-ammi, which means, "Not my people." They

[1] Gen. 34.12.
[2] Gen. 31.15.

are clearly names with a special significance, and here we need to remember that the Prophets did not rely on their words alone; they made their teaching memorable by their acts as well as their deeds. You will remember that Jeremiah carried a large earthenware pot through the streets of Jerusalem, collecting a crowd as he went, and then smashed it at the city gate to show how complete the coming destruction of Jerusalem was to be. So Hosea named his children with significant names to drive home the point of his teaching; he gave them names which point to the character of the times, which point the inheritance they had been born into in this northern kingdom at this time, which point the responsibility they would be called upon to share.

At this stage of his life it is best to see Hosea as a prophet like Amos; indeed, a prophet carrying on Amos's work of pointing out to the people the consequences of ignoring God's demands for righteousness. At this stage he had Amos's vision of a righteous God uncompromisingly demanding righteousness of his people—and at this stage he had no more than Amos's insight. So his first prophetic act was to condemn the bloodbath by which the reigning dynasty in Israel, the kings descend from Jehu, had secured their thrones. When Jehu killed King Joram, King Ahab's son, a hundred years before Hosea's time, and mounted the throne of Israel, he made sure that no descendant of Ahab could try to get the throne back again. He did it by having them all murdered and their heads brought to him in the Valley of Jezreel, in the north of Israel:

> . . . and they that brought up the children sent to Jehu, saying, We are your servants, and we will do all that you bid us. We will not make any one king: do whatever is good in your eyes. Then he wrote to them a second time saying, If you are on my side, and if you are ready to obey me, take the heads of your master's sons, and come to me at Jezreel tomorrow at this time. . . . And when the letter came to them, they took the king's sons, and slew them . . . and put their heads in baskets, and sent them to him at Jezreel.[1]

There were seventy heads in the baskets; all of those who might have endangered Jehu's crown. He had them piled in two heaps, one either side of the city gate of Jezreel, where Ahab's palace stood. The people took the hint.

So Hosea calls his first son Jezreel, to show that God had not forgotten:

> And the Lord said to him, call his name Jezreel; for yet a little while, and I will punish the house of Jehu for the blood of Jezreel, and I will put an end to the kingdom of the house of Israel.[2]

[1] 2 Kings 10.5ff. (4 Kings 10.5ff.)
[2] Hos. 1.4.

The other two names, the daughter called "She has not obtained mercy", and the son called "Not my people", are general predictions of the downfall not only of the reigning house with its blood-stained hands, but of the people as well.

Hosea had good reasons for warning that the punishment would involve the ordinary people as well; there were crimes against God both more serious and more recent than the massacre by which the ruling house gained the throne. He had more in mind the kind of worship in which the people took part at the local village shrines, the kind of religion which was woven into the texture of their daily lives.

When the Hebrews finally moved into the Promised Land after the escape from Egypt their penetration was slow and patchy. It was nothing like the lightning conquest and occupation which the Book of Joshua pictures for us. Jerusalem, to give only one example, was still in non-Hebraic hands, together with most of the centre of the country, two hundred years later when David captured it. It would be more accurate to call the Hebrew movement into Canaan an infiltration rather than a conquest. The Canaanites were farmers, growing wheat and barley in cultivated fields, mainly in the low-lying parts of the country, and at first the newly arriving Hebrews settled in the hilly parts the Canaanites had little use for. There they could continue their tradi-

tional skill of raising sheep. But the scattered
communities of Hebrews soon learned the
Canaanite agricultural techniques, and with those
techniques the Canaanite religion associated with
them. For the Canaanite economy and their
religion were bound together in what appeared to
be an indissoluble unity. It is not in the least
surprising that the Hebrews, at least in the country
districts, took over the Canaanite gods together
with the Canaanite crops, or at least found a
place for their worship alongside the worship of
their own God, Yahweh.

Those Canaanite gods (and goddesses) were
essentially fertility gods, and their worship centred
round fertility rites. Each local village had its
own local god, little more than the spirit of the
fields, and his consort. One of the Hebrew words
meaning "to marry" is *baal*, and from this comes
a word for a husband or for a lord—*baal*—and it
is this word which is used of these local gods, they
are called the *baalim*. There is more than a sug-
gestion, too, that there is a more powerful *baal*
whose authority extends over the whole country.
On these local gods hangs the fertility of the
fields and the success of the crops. The *baal* is the
source of life and all growth: the grain springs in
the earth, the cow calves, the sheep are in lamb
and the olive tree and vine bear heavily, all by
the power of the *baal*. Or, in the biblical phrase
which may well have been part of the baal rites:

"The corn and the wine and the oil increase."

Associated with each *baal* is his consort, the *ashtareth*, or in the plural form, *ashtaroth*. In the popular Canaanite belief, and soon in the popular Hebrew belief too, it was the intercourse between the *baalim* and the *ashtaroth* which brought fertility and life to their crops and stock. And, by a natural projection, health to the people and healing to the sick. In fact there was very little in the ordinary everyday lives of the people which did not depend in the end on the fertility of the *baalim* and their *ashtaroth*. So deeply did this penetrate into the minds of the people that it found a place in their language. In the Book of Deuteronomy, of all places, the very centre of the condemnation of the *baalim* and *ashtaroth* and all they stood for, the actual name of the goddess is used as a word for "offspring"; speaking of Yahweh, the God of the Hebrews, the writer says:

> And he will love you and bless you and multiply you: he will also bless . . . the increase of your cattle and the young of your flock. . . .[1]

"The young of your flock": *ashtaroth tsonecha*— there the goddess is! Yet it is quite certain that the Deuteronomist, or the later priest who wrote that particular part of Deuteronomy, was very far indeed from wishing to encourage the old

[1] Deut. 7.13.

Canaanite religious practices or any trace of them.

This was the religion of the folk who lived all round Hosea, and it would be sufficient in itself to explain his choice of language when speaking of God's attitude to the Hebrew people who took part in the *baal* worship. As the *baal* rites were fertility rites it was natural that sexual intercourse and sacred prostitution should play a large part in them. The parts of the *baal* and his *ashtoreth* were played by a priest and a priestess, and each local shrine would be the scene of the rites which ensured fertility for the district. Those shrines were usually in the gloom of a thick grove of trees, though sometimes they were on the top of a hill. Sometimes an idol would figure in the shrine, but more often it seems that a staff or pole was used as the symbol for the *baal*, and this would be erected alongside the altar. So Hosea writes:

> My people inquire of a thing of wood,
>> and their staff gives them oracles.
> For a spirit of harlotry has led them astray,
>> and they have left their God to play the
>> harlot.
> They sacrifice on the tops of mountains,
>> and make offerings upon the hills,
> under oak, poplar, and terebinth,
>> because their shade is good.
> Therefore your daughters play the harlot,
>> and your brides commit adultery.[1]

[1] Hos. 4.12f.

3

If sacred prostitution was the central feature of the *baal* rites it was natural that Hosea used the language of fornication and adultery to describe it. Yahweh the Hebrew God had chosen this people for himself, and rescued them from Egypt. So Hosea saw Yahweh as Israel's husband, and he would punish his people's apostasy as a husband punishes his wife's adultery:

> I know Ephraim, and Israel is not hid from me: for now, O Ephraim, you have played the harlot, Israel is defiled. Their deeds do not permit them to return to their God: for the spirit of harlotry is within them, and they know not the Lord. . . .

> They have dealt faithlessly with the Lord; for they have borne alien children . . .

> Ephraim shall become a desolation in the day of punishment: among the tribes of Israel I declare what is sure.[1]

Hosea had much to learn yet about this God of the Hebrews, Yahweh, whom he worshipped and whom he so passionately defended, and he was going to learn it the hard way. So far he had learned what Amos had to teach him, but no more. But before we see the great stride Hosea took in his insight into the character of God, there is one important thing to notice. The Hebrews had accepted *baal*-worship along with

[1] Hos. 5.3f,7,9.

the Canaanite skills in growing crops, because
they thought the Canaanite gods had control of
those crops. Hosea told them their mistake. It
was Yahweh, their own God, who was the true
God of the harvest, Yahweh who really brought
fertility to their fields, not the *baalim*. Not only
was their worship of the *baalim* degrading, it was
all a ghastly mistake. Their true prosperity lay
in the worship of their own God. There is a sort
of savage irony about it all:

> She did not know
>   that it was I who gave her
>   the corn, the wine, and the oil,
> and who lavished upon her silver
>   and gold which they used for Baal.
> Therefore I will take back
>   my corn in its time,
>   and my wine in its season;
> and I will take away my wool and my flax,
>   which were to cover her nakedness.
> Now I will uncover her lewdness
>   in the sight of her lovers,
>   and no-one shall rescue her out of my
>   hand. . .
> And I will lay waste her vines and her fig
>   trees,
>   of which she said,
> These are my hire,
>   which my lovers have given me.

> I will make them a forest,
> and the beasts of the field shall devour them.[1]

Not only did the power and authority of Yahweh, the Hebrew God, extend over other people and into other lands, but he was also responsible for the things which people thought were controlled by other gods. He was not just a shepherd god who could snatch his people out of Egypt and make sure that their sheep had good lambs. Nor was he only the God of battle hosts who led his people to victory. He also controlled and directed all branches of agriculture, even branches which his people did not know about when he first chose them. This further insight into the extent of Yahweh's power was another important step along the road leading to the realization that he is the only God; not just the most powerful God among the gods, but the God who made all that is and holds all in existence by the continual exercise of his creative power. It was to be long before the full realization of this sank into the heart of the ordinary Hebrew worshipper; several hundred years, in fact. But Hosea had at least made this truth more available than it was before. It is this truth the Psalmist draws on when he sings:

> Thou hast put gladness in my heart,
> Since the time that their corn and wine and oil
>   increased;

[1] Hos. 2.8–12.

I will lay me down in peace and take my rest,
For it is thou, Lord, only, that makest me dwell
in safety.[1]

But important as all this is, it is none of it the
main advance Hosea made in the Hebrew penetration into the character of their God, Yahweh.
The main thing Hosea learned about God was his
infinite patience and steadfastness and faithfulness and unchanging love for his people, even
when they were slow to respond to that love and
repeatedly betrayed it. Hosea learned this from
examining his own feelings when his wife deserted
him.

After their marriage had been going for perhaps
five years, it seems that Hosea's wife deserted him
for at least one other man. Hosea's first reaction
was one of cold anger; he says to their children:

Plead with your mother, plead;
For she is not my wife, neither am I her husband: and let her put away her harlotry from
her face, and her adulteries from between her
breasts; lest I . . . make her as a wilderness,
and set her like a dry land . . .
Behold, I will hedge up her way with thorns,
and I will make a fence against her, so that she
cannot find her paths. And she shall follow
after her lovers, but not overtake them; and
she shall seek them, but shall not find them.[2]

[1] Ps. 4.8f.
[2] Hos. 2.1ff.

This reaction of Hosea's would find more than approval from his neighbours; in fact they would be more than likely to think he was being very moderate, foolishly moderate. The contemporary law for adultery is quoted in the Book of Deuteronomy; it is brief and to the point:

If a man be found lying with the wife of another man, both of them shall die, the man who lay with the woman, and the woman: so you shall purge the evil from Israel.[1]

But when his first anger had passed he found that he could not bring himself to cast her off, still less to have her punished ruinously; rather, that he wanted her to return to him and he wanted to restore the early days of their marriage when it seemed that nothing could break it:

Behold, I will allure her, and bring her into the wilderness, and speak tenderly to her . . . and she shall answer as in the days of her youth.[2]

Hosea was surely not the first Hebrew to remain faithful to his wife even though she be unfaithful to him, nor the first to receive her back when she said:

I will go and return to my first husband; for it was better with me then than now.[3]

[1] Deut. 22.22.
[2] Hos. 2.14f.
[3] Hos. 2.7.

But he was the first who we know recognized in this experience that this was how God reacted to his people's unfaithfulness. That despite the way they followed other gods whose worship they found more congenial and less demanding, and despite their short memories of the ways their own God, Yahweh, had worked in their history and enabled them to become a nation from being a collection of Egyptian slaves; and despite the agreement, the covenant, they entered into with him, and their failure to keep it; *yet* Yahweh does not reject them and leave them to their fate. He constantly renews the opportunity to return to him. He supports and protects them, and patiently waits for them to return, and the misfortunes which happen to them as a people are not mere retributive punishment by God; they are reformative, purging, healing and cleansing punishments, meant to bring them to their senses and back to their God. It is this side of God's character that Amos did not see; and it is for this particular insight that we are indebted to Hosea.

All this Hosea worked out in the rest of the book, and if he occasionally faltered and hesitated to draw the full conclusion, who can blame him? It was a vast new dimension he had uncovered in the character of God:

When Israel was a child, I loved him,
    and out of Egypt I called my son.

The more I called them,
  the more they went from me;
they kept sacrificing to the Baals,
  and burning incense to idols.
Yet it was I who taught Ephraim to walk,
  I took them up in my arms:
    but they did not know that I healed them.
I led them with cords of compassion,
  with the bands of love,
and I became to them as one
  who eases the yoke on their jaws,
    and I bent down to them and fed them.

My people are bent on turning away from me;
  so they are appointed to the yoke,
    and none shall remove it.
How can I give you up, O Ephraim!
  How can I hand you over, O Israel! . . .
My heart recoils within me,
  my compassion grows warm and tender.
I will not execute my fierce anger,
  I will not again destroy Ephraim;
For I am God and not man,
  the Holy One is your midst,
    and I will not come to destroy.[1]

In his writings a new word appears to describe
this new dimension he has discovered in the
character of God. It is the word *hesedh*, and it
first appears in the heart of a passage where Hosea
describes God's renewal of his betrothal to his

[1] Hos. 11.1–4, 7–9.

people. The Revised Standard Version translates it by "steadfast love":

> And I will betroth you to me for ever; I will betroth you to me in righteousness, and in justice, and in steadfast love and in mercy. I will betroth you to me in faithfulness: and you shalt know the Lord.[1]

The threefold repetition of "betroth" gives it emphasis and serves, too, to underline the permanent nature of this act of restoration by Yahweh; and the righteousness and justice and steadfast love and mercy (that is, tenderness) and faithfulness, these are all the gifts Yahweh brings to his betrothed people, the character Yahweh gives to Israel, the share he gives them in his own character. A much later writer, writing about the creation of man, is going to express this in the words:

> And God created man in his own image, in the image of God he created him.[2]

This is not just a restoration, it is a restoration and a *re*-creation.

This restoration will bring with it material prosperity, for this is the God who controls the harvest and the God who brings peace or war, the Lord God of battle hosts:

[1] Hos. 2.19f.
[2] Gen. 1.27.

And in that day will I make a covenant for them with the beasts of the field, and with the birds of the air, and with the creeping things of the ground: and I will abolish the bow, the sword, and war from the land; and I will make them lie down safely.[1]

There is a hint here of the restoration of paradise, the return to the primitive purity of the Hebrews before they entered Canaan and became involved with all these agricultural gods and the temptation to desert Yahweh, their own God.

At one stage Hosea reversed every detail of his early denunciations. He started by naming his children with significant names to point the anger of God and the inevitability and completeness of the punishment he would bring to the nation. The boy Jezreel was a living reminder that the memory of unavenged blood was still alive; the other two, "She has not obtained mercy" and "Not my people", were living witnesses that because the people had broken their side of the sacred covenant God no longer felt bound by his promises. At the heart of their tradition about the Covenant God had made with them through Moses was the promise:

I will take you for my people, and I will be your God.[2]

[1] Hos. 2.18.
[2] Exod. 6.7.

That covenant promise, said the early Hosea, was ended because of Israel's unfaithfulness. But the later Hosea, the Hosea with the insight into the steadfast love of Yahweh, took it all back again, and reapplied the name Jezreel and reversed the names of his two other children.

Jezreel is the name of the valley in the north of the country which runs inland beneath Mount Carmel, but the name literally means, "Whom God soweth". Hosea took this literal meaning and applied it to Israel in her restored betrothal to God. Israel was now the nation whom God sowed in the land, the people he planted that it might grow under his care and protection, watered and fed by him. All the things on which the nation, Jezreel, depended for her prosperity would plead with God to prosper them so that the nation might prosper: the heavens which gave rain, the earth which received it and produced the corn and wine and oil which were the nation's life:

And in that day, says the Lord, I will answer the heavens, and they shall answer the earth; and the earth shall answer the corn, and the wine, and the oil; and they shall answer Jezreel. And I will sow her unto me in the land; and I will have mercy upon her that had not obtained mercy; and I will say to them which were not my people, you are my people; and they shall say, Thou art my God.[1]

[1] Hos. 2.21–4.

We do not know what the people made of
Hosea's teaching. With each of the other major
prophets of this period we are told something of
the reaction to his teaching. Not so with Hosea.
His insight was taken up and developed by Isaiah
and Jeremiah, and indeed by the authors of
Deuteronomy, but all of them in the southern kingdom, not in the northern kingdom of Israel, where
Hosea lived and taught. For Hosea was the last
voice for the northern kingdom. Only twenty years
later the kingdom was overwhelmed by the
Assyrians and dropped out of history together
with its people. We shall see something of the
events which were the immediate cause of that
destruction when we look at Isaiah in the next
chapter, for in the southern kingdom of Judah
he was intimately concerned with it all. But at
least it is worth remembering that the last voice
from the northern kingdom was the voice of Hosea
speaking of the infinite tenderness of God.

Note: Key Texts in Hosea

1.2–9; 2.2–14, 19–20; 3.1–3	His personal life
2.8–13; 4.12–13; 5.7; 13.1–3	Canaanite religion background of worship of Baalim
4.1–2,11; 7.1–10; 10.4	Social sins and wrongs
5.8–15; 9.7–17	Destruction of Israel

7.11–12,16; 8.7–9; 9.3,6; 10.6; 11.1–7; 12.1	Condemnation of foreign alliances
4.6–9	Sins of the priests
5.15; 6.1–3; 10.10–12; 11.9–11; all of ch. 14	Punishment as remedial, leaving a purged remnant
11.1–4; 12.9; 13.4–6	Mention of the Exodus from Egypt
2.18,21–3	God brings prosperity
	"Hesedh"
2.19	"Steadfast love"
4.1	"Kindness"
6.4	"Love"
6.6	"Steadfast love"
10.12	"Steadfast love"
12.6	"Love"
	Memorable phrases
8.7	"For they sow the wind, and they shall reap the whirlwind."
11.4	"I drew them with cords of compassion, with bands of love."
13.14	"I will ransom them from the power of the grave; I will redeem them from death: O death, where are thy plagues? O grave, where is thy destruction?"

4

ISAIAH

THERE is an important problem we must solve before we can start to study Isaiah. It is the problem of what in fact the Isaiah *we* know about, the Isaiah who lived and taught at the end of the eighth century BC in Judah, *did* write. For one thing is certain: he did not write all of the book which bears his name in the Old Testament. Some of that book is his, but much of it was written by other people.

It may be a help if we take a quick look at the way in which the Old Testament has been handed down to us, the way it reached its present form. Books as we now know them, made of separate sheets folded and sewn together and bound between covers, are a comparatively modern invention and this has only been the normal way of making them for perhaps a little over a thousand years. Before that, and certainly from Isaiah's time right through the Old-Testament and New-Testament times, books were handwritten on scrolls, rolls of writing material. Sometimes specially prepared sheepskin was used, parchment; sometimes the very tough Egyptian paper, called papyrus from the name of the Nile reed used in the making of it; and sometimes even a thinly beaten-out sheet of copper. Copper scrolls have been discovered in the last ten years near the Dead Sea, and the greatest care and ingenuity has had to be taken in opening them after all these years; they date from the first century BC, and one of them has a copy of the Book of Isaiah written on it.

Isaiah taught and wrote about the years 740–700 BC, and his writings would be available to later generations through the work of the scribes, the men who made careful copies of important books. By about the year 200 BC there were a number of these prophetic books and, of course, other books of what we now call the Old Testament, and it was decided to collect them together. The prophetic writings were all gathered together and written onto four papyrus scrolls, and it is at this point that it is easy to see how some of the writings of other prophets than Isaiah could get attached to his own writings. With two of the scrolls, the ones containing the books of Jeremiah and Ezekiel, there is not too much of a problem: the books were about big enough for each to fill one scroll. There is not much of a problem about the minor prophets either, the twelve short books from Hosea to Malachi at the end of the Old Testament; they fitted comfortably onto one scroll. It is with the fourth scroll that our present problem started. It looks as if the original writings of Isaiah only took up the first part of the scroll, leaving most of it empty. The normal length for a papyrus scroll was about thirty feet, and it would be about ten inches broad. When the scribe had finished copying Isaiah he found he had about twenty feet left, and he used those twenty feet as a convenient space to copy various prophetic fragments of teaching and at least one other prophetic work of major importance: the anonymous prophet who wrote somewhere between 540 and 522, just at the end of the Hebrew exile in Babylon. It is only too easy to see then how a later scribe could make the mistake of thinking that everything written on this scroll was by Isaiah, instead of only the first ten feet of it.

What part of this book, then, do we need to study to find the mind and teaching of the prophet Isaiah we know about? Well, we can leave out chs. 40–66: they clearly belong to a period two hundred years later than our Isaiah, for they mention Cyrus, King of Persia, who overthrew the Babylonian Empire and released the Hebrews from their captivity and allowed those who wanted to to go back home again. That leaves chs. 1–39. These chapters, again, were not originally one book but a collection of small books written at different times and then edited by successive generations.

Of these books chs. 1–12 constitute the main book of Isaiah's teaching at various stages in his life, and chs. 36–9 are an almost word-for-word quotation of chs. 18–20 of 2 Kings, chapters which describe an invasion of Judah by the Assyrians in which Isaiah was closely involved as adviser to the King. So we shall concentrate on chs. 1–12 and 36–9.

Isaiah lived during a period of great stirrings and political upheaval. He lived to see the northern kingdom crushed and its people scattered, never again to appear in history; and towards the end of his life he saw the same great power, Assyria, camped round Jerusalem with all the rest of Judah overrun by it; and also knew the relief when they withdrew without capturing the city.

For years the potentially great power of Assyria, with its capital at Nineveh, had brooded to the north of Palestine, but Israel and Judah had ignored it. Indeed, if they had but realized it, much of their prosperity was indirectly due to Assyria. From a period starting about a hundred years before Isaiah's time the Assyrians had been thinking about the land just north of the Hebrews, the land of Syria with its capital at Damascus, and in 841 and 838, and again in 800, Assyrian armies marched down to Damascus and subdued the country and made the people pay a large tribute of gold and silver and merchandise. Israel and Judah had benefited from this, for while Damascus was busy keeping the Assyrians satisfied, they couldn't trouble their Hebrew neighbours in the south. The Hebrews enjoyed a golden age of prosperity which none of the warnings of Amos and Hosea could disturb.

But in 745 all this changed. To the Assyrian throne in Nineveh came Tiglath-Pileser III, the first of the long line of dynamic personalities and great soldiers who were to rule Assyria and the whole of the Middle East for 120 years. Tiglath-Pileser set out to conquer and create a great empire. To do this it was essential that he secure Palestine: Palestine rich in wood and metals, with its long coastline and, above all, the only sure route to Egypt, and the only one practicable for an army which must be fed by the country through which it was marching. For the Hebrews political independence ended at a stroke and, except for a brief period hundreds of years later, they never regained it. Never regained it, that is, until our own time—1948. World history overtook the Hebrews in 738 BC and from then onwards they were controlled by it.

Of those who submitted to her power, Assyria demanded large sums to be paid as tribute, and by this means she not only enriched herself and paid for the support of her armies, but she also

made sure that her conquered neighbours would
be too impoverished to be able to mount any
effective resistance. If there *was* resistance, then
the Assyrians had discovered a new method of
crushing it. The method was to take the dictum
"divide and rule" to its furthest extreme. Any
country which refused to submit to Assyrian
demands found its people deported, and not
deported in any single group where the national
identity might be maintained, but scattered
throughout the Assyrian Empire, and other people
brought in to take their place. It was very effective. Israel and Judah were swift to submit and
their names occur in the inscriptions Tiglath-
Pileser has left, recording his conquest. Amongst
the things he demanded from them, he says, were:

> . . . gold, silver, tin, iron, antimony, linen
> garments with multicoloured trimmings, gar-
> ments of their native dark purple wool, all
> kinds of costly objects be they products of the
> sea or of the continent, the choice products
> of their regions, the treasures of their kings,
> horses and mules trained for the yoke.[1]

There would be few among the people, merchant,
farmer, town-dweller or peasant, who would not
feel the burden when the tribute was gathered.
And the tribute did not stop at material things;
it was a spiritual tribute as well, involving the
worship of the Assyrian gods:

[1] J. B. Pritchard, *The Ancient Near East* (1954), p. 193.

As to Hanno of Gaza [one of the Philistine towns]
who had fled before my army and run away to
Egypt, I conquered the town of Gaza, and took
all his personal property; and I placed the
images of my gods and my royal image in his
own palace and declared them to be thenceforward the gods of their country. I imposed upon
them tribute.[1]

We shall have occasion to remember this later,
when we trace the consequences of King Ahaz's
refusal to listen to Isaiah.

It was against this background that Isaiah first
appeared. He describes in ch. 6 the circumstances
of the vision or spiritual experience which inaugurated his ministry; it occurred about the year
740 BC, just about the time Hosea was teaching
of the tender loving kindness of God in the
northern kingdom; the setting is the Temple in
Jerusalem:

In the year that King Uzziah died I saw the
Lord sitting upon a throne, high and lifted up,
and his train filled the temple. Above him
stood the seraphim: each had six wings; with
two he covered his face, and with two he
covered his feet, and with two he flew. And one
called to another and said, Holy, holy, holy, is
the Lord of hosts: the whole earth is full of his
glory. And the foundations of the thresholds

[1] Pritchard, p. 194.

shook at the voice of him who called, and the
house was filled with smoke.[1]

He then tells of his own fears of unworthiness, and
then of being purged of his sins, and then of the
command which started his ministry:

And I heard the voice of the Lord, saying,
Whom shall I send, and who will go for us?
Then I said, Here I am, send me. And he said
Go . . .[2]

Isaiah entered into his ministry with no illusions
about certain success. He was a native of Jerusalem, familiar with the corruption of the capital
of a rich country, and with acute political insight.
He realized that he was no more likely to be
successful in the southern kingdom of Judah, than
Amos was successful in the northern kingdom.
And in the colonial methods of Assyria he saw
the pattern of his country's future history: his
people would refuse to live the kind of life their
God expected, and the more they turned from
him the less they would be able to obey him, and
in the end they would be overwhelmed by Assyria
just as they had seen other countries overwhelmed:

And he said, Go, and say to this people:
Hear and hear, but do not understand;
see and see, but do not perceive.

[1] Isa. 6.1–4.
[2] Isa. 6.8–9a.

Make the heart of this people fat,
  and their ears heavy,
  and shut their eyes;
lest they see with their eyes,
  and hear with their ears,
and understand with their hearts,
  and turn and be healed.
Then I said, How long, O Lord? And he said:
Until cities lie waste
  without inhabitant,
and houses without men,
  and the land is utterly desolate.[1]

It is not a very heartening picture.

At this stage of his life Isaiah was full of the punishment which he felt must be the inevitable result of the injustice, luxury and sacrilege he saw all round him in Jerusalem. So although his denunciations were not so sweeping as those of Amos only a few years earlier, and although the promise of a remnant which would survive the punishment was already there, yet Isaiah at this time fits naturally into the same pattern as Amos, doing for the southern kingdom what Amos had already done for the northern one:

The Lord enters into judgement
  with the elders and princes of his people:
It is you who have devoured the vineyard,
  the spoil of the poor is in your houses.

[1] Isa. 6.9–11.

What do you mean by crushing my people,
   by grinding the face of the poor?[1]

And the rich women of Jerusalem do not escape
his attention:
   The Lord said:
   Because the daughters of Zion are haughty
     and walk with outstretched necks,
     glancing wantonly along as they go,
   mincing along as they go,
     tinkling with their feet; . . .
   In that day the Lord will take away the finery
   of the anklets, the headbands and the crescents;
   the pendants, the bracelets and the scarves; the
   headdresses, the armlets, the sashes. . .[2]

and so on for several more verses. It is a very
vivid picture Isaiah gives of the Jerusalem people
whose only concern was to be well ahead of the
latest fashion—and who weren't particularly
worried how the money had been obtained.

But just as Amos had seen the plumbline of
God set in the midst of the northern kingdom, so
now Isaiah saw the majesty of God reigning from
the Temple in the midst of Jerusalem, and he drew
much the same conclusion. By this standard and
presence the people will be judged:

Enter into the rock and hide in the dust, from
before the terror of the Lord, and from the

[1] Isa. 3.14f.
[2] Isa. 3.16,18ff.

glory of his majesty. The lofty looks of man shall be brought low, and the haughtiness of men shall be bowed down, and the Lord alone shall be exalted in that day.[1]

But even so, it will be a just punishment, not an indiscriminate one, and those who are blameless will escape to form the purged and holy remnant:

He that is left in Zion, and remains in Jerusalem, shall be called holy, every one that is written among the living in Jerusalem: when the Lord shall have washed away the filth of the daughters of Zion, and shall have purged the blood of Jerusalem from its midst by a spirit of judgement and by a spirit of burning.[2]

It was during this time that a son was born to Isaiah, and, following a practice with which we are already familar from Hosea, he gave him a significant name. He named him Shear-Jashub, which means, "A remnant shall return." It is a name which contains within it both a warning and a promise, a warning that there is a punishment coming which will destroy many of the people, yet also a promise that the destruction will not be complete; there will be a remnant saved who will still be the beloved of God.

Had this been the sum total of Isaiah's teach-

[1] Isa. 2.10–11.
[2] Isa. 4.3f.

ing there would not have been anything particularly remarkable about it, but now the march of political events forced him to reapply his vision of God's presence at a much deeper level.

In 735 the king died and Ahaz mounted the throne of Judah. Meanwhile the northern kingdom, Israel, and her northern neighbour, Syria, with its capital at Damascus, decided that the time had come to throw off all Assyrian control and reassert their independence. It was a suicidal move, but at the time Tiglath-Pileser had his hands full keeping control of parts of his empire far away from Palestine. Israel and Syria formed an alliance to revolt against Assyria, and to make themselves stronger they tried to draw Judah into it as well. When Judah wisely refused to have any part in it the Syrians and the Israelis, under their kings, Rezin and Pekah, marched on Jerusalem, and when they could not capture it sat down to a full-scale siege. It is easy to imagine how worried king and people were:

In the days of Ahaz the son of Jotham, son of Uzziah, king of Judah, Rezin the king of Syria, and Pekah the son of Remaliah, king of Israel, went up to Jerusalem to war against it; but could not prevail against it. And it was told the house of David, Syria is in league with Ephraim. And his heart and the heart of his people shook as the trees of the forest are moved with the wind.[1]

[1] Isa. 7.1f.

It was at this point that Isaiah appeared to advise the king.

Isaiah's advice was brief: it was to sit tight and trust God and do nothing but wait. Out of the certainty of his experience of the presence of God in the midst of Jerusalem Isaiah now drew the conclusion that if Judah trusted in that presence alone she would come to no harm. It was hard advice, and Isaiah reinforced its impact with the name of his son: Shear-Jashub: God will not let his people perish, a remnant will be left to return:

> And the Lord said to Isaiah, Go forth to meet Ahaz, you and Shear-Jashub your son, at the end of the conduit of the upper pool on the highway to the Fuller's Field, and say to him, Take heed, be quiet, do not fear, and do not let your heart be faint because of these two smouldering stumps of firebrands, at the fierce anger of Rezin and Syria and the son of Remaliah . . . saying, Let us go up against Judah and terrify it, and let us conquer it for ourselves. . .
> Thus says the Lord God:
> It shall not stand,
> and it shall not come to pass.[1]

But standing there on the city wall, by the main water supply, and looking down on the hostile army surrounding the city, it seemed to King

---

[1] Isa. 7.3ff.

Ahaz that it was only too likely to come to pass. He refused to see the besieging kings as spent fires, burnt out and only faintly smoking. So he hesitated, unconvinced by Isaiah's policy of doing nothing. In his mind there was another plan; he was a vassal of Assyria and these men camped round his walls were revolting against Assyria. Why not send to Assyria for help, send an even larger sum than was called for in the tribute and ask for an Assyrian army to come quickly and relieve Jerusalem and punish the revolt of Israel and Syria? To the king it seemed a very clever way out.

While he was hesitating Isaiah tried another way of convincing Ahaz that it was God's will that he do nothing, and certainly not call in the Assyrians. Isaiah invited Ahaz to ask for a proof, any proof he liked that would convince him that what he said was the word of God. But Ahaz did not want to be convinced; his mind was made up:

> And the Lord spake again unto Ahaz, Ask a sign of the Lord your God; ask it either in the depth, or in the height above. But Ahaz said, I will not ask, and I will not put the Lord to the test.[1]

And so Isaiah realized that he had failed to turn the king away from his disastrous plan.

But Ahaz was not to be allowed to get away with it; whether he wanted it or not he was going

[1] Isa. 7.10–12.

to have a sign, and it was a sign which came right out of the vision Isaiah had seen in the Temple years before. That vision had been of the presence of God in the midst of his people. So now Isaiah gave Ahaz the sign of Immanuel: the boy who would be born of a young woman very soon and who would be named Immanuel, "God with us."

Now let me repeat that we are concerned at present *only* to try and see what Isaiah meant by this and what Ahaz and the people standing round him in the fuller's field were expected to mean by it. Our immediate task is not to see this in the context of Christmas and the birth of Jesus Christ, but to see it against the background of eighth-century Jerusalem, and an army around the walls, and the determination of the king to call in Assyria to help him and Isaiah's warning that this policy is disastrous. There has been a great deal of discussion of this passage, of course, but seen in its context it tries to tell the king two things. God is with us, says Isaiah to the king, and two consequences flow from this: First, the countries of the two kings who are attacking Jerusalem are going to be devastated. How soon, Isaiah is not absolutely sure, but it will be before this boy about to be born is old enough to know the difference between right and wrong. Israel and Syria are going to be destroyed fairly soon:

Therefore the Lord himself will give you a sign; behold a virgin shall conceive and bear a son,

and shall call his name Immanuel. . . . For before the child knows how to refuse the evil, and
choose the good, the land before whose two
kings you are in dread will be deserted.[1]

That is the first consequence: God will deliver
his people from their enemies. But the second consequence of God's presence will be that Judah will
also be involved in destruction. They have refused
to trust in God alone; they are calling in Assyria
to help them; they will find that Assyria will in
the end devastate them as well. This too is contained in the Immanuel prophecy of Isaiah, for he
says that by the time Immanuel has reached years
of discretion he will find himself having to live
on the food of the wilderness, on wild honey and
curds: the food of nomad shepherds, not of
settled town-dwellers:

Curds and honey shall he eat when he knows
how to refuse the evil and choose the good.[2]

All this is carefully expanded and underlined
by Isaiah, so we are not dependent on a chance
interpretation just of the Immanuel passage.
Isaiah drives it all home by begetting another
son himself and calling him by the significant
name *Maher Shalal Hash Baz*, which means, "The
Spoil Speeds, the Prey Hastens." It is a further
warning of imminent invasion and defeat at the

[1] Isa. 7.14,16.
[2] Isa. 7.15.

hands of Assyria. Isaiah was careful to do all he
could to draw attention to this second son of his;
he publicly announced that he was going to beget
a son, he wrote the name in the common script
of the people and large enough for all to see, and
he had it formally witnessed by the chief priest
and another court official:

> Then the Lord said to me, Take a large tablet
> and write upon it in common characters, Be-
> longing to Maher-Shalal-Hash-Baz. And I got
> reliable witnesses, Uriah the priest and Zecha-
> riah the son of Jeberechiah, to attest for me.
> And I went to the prophetess, and she con-
> ceived and bore a son. Then the Lord said to
> me, Call his name Maher-Shalal-Hash-Baz; for
> before the child knows how to cry My father, or
> My mother, the wealth of Damascus [i.e.,
> Syria] and the spoil of Samaria [i.e., Israel, the
> northern of the two Hebrew kingdoms] will be
> carried away before the king of Assyria.[1]

Now all that is straightforward, but what is of
importance is that Isaiah went on to include
Judah in this warning, and at the same time tie
Judah's warning into the Immanuel prophecy.
He says:

> Behold, the Lord is bringing up against them
> [Syria and Israel] the waters of the River,
> mighty and many, the king of Assyria and all
> his glory; and it will rise over all its channels

[1] Isa. 8.1–4.

and go over all its banks; and it will sweep on into Judah, it will overflow and pass on, reaching even to the neck; and its outspread wings will fill the breadth of your land, O Immanuel.[1]

Immanuel's land is going to be involved in the devastation. God is with them but this is going to bring them punishment for disobeying him and refusing to trust him, even if they are at first saved from their immediate danger.

Ahaz sent to Tiglath-Pileser, and stripped the Temple of its treasure to buy Assyrian help, but he also paid a price beyond any material reckoning; he erected an Assyrian altar in the very Temple itself and introduced Assyrian worship at which he himself officiated. In return the Assyrians destroyed both Syria and Israel. Israel was the first to be attacked, and part of her population was deported and most of the country turned into Assyrian provinces with Assyrian governors. Syria went the same way two years later. Tiglath-Pileser records his punishment of Israel:

Israel I conquered with all its inhabitants and their possessions I led to Assyria. They overthrew their king Pekah and I placed Hoshea as king over them. I received from them 10 talents of gold, 1000 talents of silver as their tribute and brought them to Assyria.[2]

[1] Isa. 8.7–8.
[2] Pritchard, p. 194.

They were considerable sums of money. The Mesopotamian talent weighed 130 lb, so Tiglath-Pileser took 1,300 lb of gold and 130,000 lb of silver from the northern kingdom. The whole country must have been ruined.

Even so the remains of the northern kingdom struggled on until Tiglath-Pileser died five years later in 727, and they then seized their chance and revolted. At first the Assyrian government was too occupied making sure of its own position, but as soon as it felt secure it moved again against Israel. This time there was to be no mistake made; the people were removed and others brought in. Again we have the testimony of the Assyrian royal records to tell us what happened:

> I besieged and conquered the town of the Samarians. I led away as prisoners 27,290 inhabitants of it and equipped from among them soldiers to man 50 chariots for my royal corps. The town I rebuilt better than it was before and settled therein people from countries which I myself had conquered. I placed an officer of mine as governor over them and imposed upon them tribute as for Assyrian citizens.[1]

So Israel disappeared from history into the anonymity of Assyrian slavery or service in the Assyrian army. It is one of the savage ironies of history that it was their brethren of the southern kingdom of Judah who brought this upon them.

[1] Pritchard, p. 195.

Israel's destruction had come just as Isaiah had realized it would, for in any event a handful of small kingdoms could be no match for Assyria. But he was mistaken in his warnings about Judah. Fall she did, and Immanuel's land was indeed a desolation, but not for another 140 years, not until the great Assyrian Empire itself had been overthrown by the Babylonians. Yet it was a very near thing, and Isaiah's prophecy all but came about as he had said it would. For the king who followed Ahaz to the throne, Hezekiah, was persuaded to join a coalition to revolt against Assyria.

Again Assyria moved swiftly and in 701 Jerusalem again found a hostile army camped round its walls; this time not the comparatively small army of their northern neighbours, but a full and victorious Assyrian army under the direction of the Assyrian General Staff. The Assyrian records state that 200,150 people were captured in the campaign which reduced forty-six of the Judaean walled towns and brought the army to the walls of Jerusalem.[1]

Isaiah's message to King Hezekiah was in effect the same as his message to Ahaz more than thirty years earlier: to do nothing but trust in God:

Thus says the Lord concerning the king of Assyria: He shall not come into this city, or shoot an arrow there, or come before it with a

[1] Pritchard, p. 200.

4

shield, or cast up a siege-mound against it. By
the way that he came, by the same shall he
return, and he shall not come into this city,
says the Lord. For I will defend this city to
save it, for my own sake, and for my servant
David's sake.[1]

The Second Book of Kings recounts how some
kind of plague swept through the encamped
Assyrians and forced them to withdraw. Naturally
the Assyrian records make no mention of this, and
in fact they say that Hezekiah paid a very heavy
tribute to the Assyrian king: 3,900 lb of gold and
104,000 lb of silver. But it *is* significant that,
although the Assyrian records specifically say
whenever other towns are captured, there is no
mention of the actual capture of Jerusalem.
Perhaps there is truth in both accounts: that the
Assyrians had to withdraw before their siege was
successful and perhaps also Hezekiah thought it
wise to make his peace with the Assyrian king
and send tribute in case he decided to return and
complete the job.

It only remains to say a word about Isaiah's
messianic teaching. Although the Old-Testament
teaching about the Messiah centres round an ideal
king who will restore the fortunes of the Hebrew
people, there are many factors which contribute
to the complete concept: the restoration of para-

[1] 2 Kings 19.32–4 (4 Kings) (=Isa. 37.33–5).

dise; the gift of a new heart and a new spirit; the Hebrews as the Bride of their God; Jerusalem as the centre of a new kingdom; the triumphant restoration of the remnant of the people. Many of these aspects find their first explicit statement in Isaiah. Such passages spring to mind as:

> For to us a child is born, to us a son is given; and the government shall be upon his shoulder; and his name shall be called Wonderful Counsellor, Mighty God, Everlasting Father, Prince of Peace. Of the increase of his government and of peace there shall be no end, upon the throne of David, and upon his kingdom, to establish it, and to uphold it with justice and with righteousness from this time forth and for evermore.[1]

Isaiah is full of the significance of the presence of Yahweh, the Hebrew's God, in the midst of them. And although this brings with it condemnation for all who have in any way betrayed that presence and refused to acknowledge and trust in it, at the same time it is the guarantee that those who merit God's favour will not be called on to share in the punishment of the rest. Nor is it possible to think that God's plans for his chosen people can be ultimately defeated even by those whom he has chosen. As it became evident to men like Isaiah that his people had no political future as pygmies

[1] Isa. 9.6–7.

in the contemporary struggles of such giant
nations as Assyria and Egypt, so at the same
time there emerged a belief that somewhere in the
far future, after all the present troubles were over,
there would dawn an age when all men would
see unmistakeably that Yahweh, the God of the
Hebrews, really is in control of it all, and really
is the only answer to all their deepest desires. Then
the messianic age would come, and Jerusalem and
the Hebrews would be at the centre of it.

In his vision of God Isaiah was above all impressed by God's holiness; his withdrawal from
anything in the least unrighteous or unworthy of
his presence. It is that holiness of God's which
Isaiah saw expressed and preserved in the remnant of the people fit to survive into the messianic
age.

NOTE: KEY TEXTS IN ISAIAH, *Chapters 1–12*

2 Kings 16–20; Isaiah 36–9	Historical background
6; 8.18	Isaiah's call
7.3; 8.3–4	Children
7.14–23; 8.8	Immanuel
6; 2.10–17; 2.19–21	Majesty of God
3.14–24; 5.1–24; 10.1–4	Social wrongs
	Religious wrongs
1.10–17	Destruction and punishment,
3.1–8; 5.25–30; 7.14–25; 8.19–22; 9.8–21; 10.20	involving first Israel and then Judah

The Remnant is one of the complex of ideas which, in various combinations, form the concept of the Messiah and the messianic age.

5

DEUTERONOMY

I T is not often in the Bible that we have a
record of the first impact made by one of the
biblical books on the people when they are
first introduced to it. But we have such a record
for the Book of Deuteronomy. It was discovered
during Josiah's reign in Judah, after the northern
kingdom had been destroyed, and it was discovered in the Temple while repairs were being
done to the fabric:

> And Hilkiah the high priest said to Shaphan the
> secretary, I have found the book of the law in
> the house of the Lord. And Hilkiah delivered
> the book to Shaphan and he read it. And Sha-
> phan the scribe told the king, saying, Hilkiah
> the priest has given me a book. And Shaphan
> read it before the king. And when the king
> heard the words of the book of the law, he rent
> his clothes.[1]

The year was 621 BC, and this discovery marked
the beginning of the last attempt of Judah to

[1] 2 Kings 22.8,10–11. (4 Kings.)

recover and establish something of her national integrity and her national religion. It was a brave attempt, but at any rate so far as short-term results go, it was not successful. Yet it was this reform, and the Book of Deuteronomy, which was its inspiration and spring, which created Judaism and made it the force which has left such a deep mark on the world. More than any other single work, it was this which made the Old Testament what it is, and which gave shape to the nationalism from which the State of Israel has sprung 2,570 years later.

But we are not primarily concerned with later history. We must first find what actually happened; how Deuteronomy came to be written, what the author or authors were trying to do for their own times and their own country, what forces and ideas and hopes shaped it. We must first try to find what happened in 621 and the years leading up to it, and try to enter into it.

Let us look, then, at the years from 700 until the great religious stir of 621. For at least the first fifty of these years the scene was dominated by the empire of Assyria, at its greatest both in power and in the area it commanded. Indeed, the scene was not merely *dominated* by Assyria: it *was* Assyria. The impetus Tiglath-Pileser had given to conquest from 745 until his death in 727 had been maintained and its pace was increased by king after king on the Assyrian throne, until the whole area east of the Mediterranean, from the mountain ranges north of Mesopotamia right through into Egypt, was in an iron grip. The northern Hebrew kingdom of Israel Assyria destroyed once and for all in 722, the southern kingdom, Judah, survived only by paying a series of crushing tributes and losing all practical political independence.

In 692 Manasseh came to the throne of Judah at the age of twelve and reigned there for fifty-five years. During those years the country sank into a morass of religious apathy and aberration. We have seen how political subjection to Assyria carried with it religious subjection as well. In the early years of Isaiah, the Judaean king, Ahaz, had ordered the erection of an Assyrian altar in the Temple in Jerusalem. He probably had no choice if he wanted Assyrian aid for the ruin of his northern neighbour, Israel, and he did all that he could desire in that direction. And we know from Tiglath-Pileser's own Assyrian records that he imposed the Assyrian gods on those whom he conquered. Already the Hebrews had gone far in accepting the local fertility gods and goddesses, the *baalim* and *ashtaroth* of the native Canaanites, with their local sanctuaries in woods and on hills. But the arrival of the Assyrian cult with its four chief gods and its nine hundred minor ones opened the floodgates. The Prophets, from Elijah to Isaiah, had fought against the cult of the *baalim*, and with some success, but now any god or religious rite which took anyone's fancy could find a place in Judah's worship. Although human sacrifice did not play a part in the Assyrian worship there were near neighbours of Judah, Moab and Ammon, whose gods Chemosh and Moleck demanded the sacrifice of boys burned alive. Once the religious defences of Judah were down this and other foreign practices rushed in. Ahaz erected an Assyrian altar in the Temple and Ahaz was the first King of Judah to sacrifice his son by fire.[1] Manasseh, whose long reign was the setting of Deuteronomy, continued the practice, and with much else:

> He built again the high places which Hezekiah his father had destroyed; and he built altars for Baal, and made an Asherah, . . . and worshipped all the host of heaven, and served them. And he built altars in the house of the Lord, of which the Lord had said, In Jerusalem will I put my name. And he built altars for all the host of heaven in the two courts of the house of the Lord, and he burned his son as an offering.[2]

And so on for verse after verse of the Second Book of Kings. Little wonder that the author of the Books of Kings turns prophet at the end of his

[1] 2 Kings 16.3. (4 Kings 16.3.)
[2] 2 Kings 21.3–6. (4 Kings 21.3–6.)

account of Manasseh's religious wrongs and
writes:

> Therefore thus says the Lord, the God of Israel,
> Behold I bring such evil upon Jerusalem and
> Judah, that whosoever hears it, his ears shall
> tingle . . . and I will wipe Jerusalem as one
> wipes a dish, wiping it and turning it upside
> down.[1]

It is remarkable that anything religious survived at all; yet out of this situation there emerged
a breathtaking vision of the majesty and universal
authority of God, concerned with every detail
of ordinary life and with every member of the
society from the king down to the least foreign
slave; a vision which has its centre in Deuteronomy.

The book was the work of a lawyer or a group
of lawyers working during the long reign of
Manasseh. We do not even know the name or
names involved in its production. The work is
such a close-knit unity that it may well be the
product of one man's mind, but in any case if a
school of lawyers produced it they must have
been bound together in as close a unity themselves, as is shown in the book. For Deuteronomy
is more than a collection and systematic codification of most of the law, common, civil and
criminal, in use by the Hebrews in Judah; it is a

[1] 2 Kings 21.12f (4 Kings 21.12f.)

codification with a purpose, and that purpose is to expound the character of the Hebrew God, Yahweh, and show how that character must find detailed expression in the lives of those who are his people and claim his love and protection. It takes the whole vast achievement of the prophets of the previous century, Amos, Hosea and Isaiah; it takes what they had to say about God and it turns that prophetic experience of God into legislation. It translates vision into law, or rather, it takes the law of the country, laws with which the people were already familiar in their everyday lives, and it shows how those familiar laws can be used as a way of expressing the holiness and righteousness and steadfast mercy and love of God in the humdrum detail of daily life. It takes the body of Hebrew law and breathes into it the life of God, so that obedience to the law is no longer just a social convenience and a reluctant price paid for the security of social relations; obedience to law becomes a way of worshipping God, a way of acknowledging his presence in the midst of the society and his concern for every detail of its life. Let us look then, in more detail, at what this group of lawyers did, lest these claims seem gravely exaggerated.

The Book of Deuteronomy passed through five stages, stretching over two hundred years, before it reached the form in which we know it now. Fortunately we are only here concerned with the first stage, the parts discovered in the Temple in 621, the parts written during Manasseh's reign; and, doubly fortunate, those parts are by far the greater bulk of the book. Successive editors later added bits and pieces, but they left intact the main bulk with which we are concerned. The part written and compiled during Manasseh's reign falls into three sections; first, there is an introduction comprising chs. 4.44–8.20 and 10.12–11.25; secondly, there is the great central collection of laws with some explanatory comments added amongst them; this section is chs. 12–26; finally there is a conclusion summing it all up, this is ch. 28.1–29.1. Let us start by looking at the materials the Deuteronomic school had to work with, the laws in use in Judah during the first part of the seventh century BC.

All societies have some kind of law, and if they have been in existence for some time their laws will date from different periods in their history. The laws in force here in Great Britain today were not all passed in one day or even during the life of one Parliament; they are the product of successive periods of the long history of the country.

So, too, with the body of Hebrew law. It was the accumulated result of centuries of legislation and experience in settling disputes and protecting the society from those who would damage it, and some of the laws were even pre-Hebraic (in the sense we are using the word "Hebrew"), the law of the people whom the Hebrews found in Canaan when they entered it after the escape from Egypt, law which the Hebrews adopted for themselves, along with the Canaanite agricultural techniques, and added to their own tribal law. By the seventh century, Manasseh's reign, there was a considerable body of law in use in Hebrew society, and the period in the nation's history when each section came into use has left its mark on the language in which the Law is written, so it is possible to separate out the various sections with some accuracy. This detective work is much helped by the discoveries of codes of law from neighbouring peoples, particularly the Assyrians and Hittites and early Babylonians, who conveniently dated their copies of their laws. And it is also helped by the reverence the Hebrew lawyers felt for the form and letter of the laws: when they collected them together they tended to copy each section much as they found it with little alteration, even if it was in archaic language. So there is not too much difficulty in finding to which period each section of law belongs, at any rate for quite a lot of the laws. This collection of laws is to be found in chs. 12–26 of Deuteronomy. Eleven groups of laws or quasi-legal traditions can be separated with some confidence, and from them it is possible to see what materials the Deuteronomic lawyers had available and what they did with it.

First there are laws which the Hebrews probably found already in use in Canaan when they moved in. These comprise on the one hand a collection of case law; precedents accumulated over the years, and bearing a remarkable similarity both in form, content and arrangement, to the great ancient Babylonian code of Hammurabi, dated about 1800 BC, over a thousand years before Deuteronomy. Typical is the law of inheritance, which lays down that a man may not favour his younger son before his elder son, where they have been born of different wives:

> If a man has two wives, the one loved and the other disliked, and they have borne him children, both the loved and the disliked, and if the first-born son is hers that is disliked, then on the day when he assigns his possessions as an inheritance to his sons, he may not treat the son of the loved as the first-born in preference to the son of the disliked, who is the first-born, but he shall acknowledge the first-born, the son of the disliked, by giving him a double portion of all that he has, for he is the first issue of his strength; the right of the first-born is his.[1]

Twenty-one topics are dealt with in this way, topics which have clearly occurred in the day-to-day business of the village courts where a body of precedents has been the guide for judgement.

[1] Deut. 21.15ff.

Also taken over from the Canaanites and adapted for Hebrew use is a set of ten rules about feasts and sacrifices. These form the core on which the Hebrew regulations for the Temple ritual grew, and they are sometimes called the ritual decalogue. In particular, and most importantly, they give directions about the three Canaanite agricultural feasts for the barley harvest, the wheat harvest, and the final feast at the end of the year when the grape harvest was complete. The Hebrew lawyers tied this system into the native Hebrew feast of Passover, and so connected the agricultural year with the escape from Egypt; an important step in the fight for the universal jurisdiction of the Hebrew God, Yahweh, over all aspects of the country's life, in place of the multitude of local fertility gods and goddesses.

The only section of law which can be assigned with any confidence to the Hebrews before they entered Canaan is the grim *lex talionis*:

Thine eye shall not pity; life shall go for life, eye for eye, tooth for tooth, hand for hand, foot for foot.[1]

(Talionis comes from the Latin *talis* = like. It may have merciful intention in *limiting* the extent of revenge for injury.) Then there are various sets of laws which could have arisen at any point after the nation found its feet and achieved stability

[1] Deut. 19.21.

under the monarchy from David onwards, any time from about 1000 BC to 800. There are instructions for judges, forbidding them to take bribes or give unjust judgements, and laying down that all men are equal before the Law. Further sections state the conditions for membership of the Full Assembly, the recognition of those who may be considered Hebrews, and forbid what are regarded as unnatural practices such as men wearing women's clothes, or the endangering of the crop by planting two different strains in the same field.

Then, moving closer to Manasseh's own times, there are laws forbidding the use of the symbols of the *baal* cults, the Asherah and the pillar or stock, and forbidding the use of blemished victims for sacrifice. Other laws deal with the problems of false prophets who support gods other than Yahweh, and there is careful regulation of the king's authority and his personal life so that he may not get above himself or get any ideas about being an absolute monarch with arbitrary powers or claims to worship.

It is an interesting collection, but there is nothing particularly remarkable about the laws themselves, nor anything which might lead us to think they are all that different from the laws of neighbouring countries. On the one hand, perhaps they are more daring in their claims to control the king, but on the other hand, in some sections they are more harsh than some of the surrounding codes, even ones which are possibly a lot older.

No, the truly remarkable feature is the explanatory framework in which they were set by the Deuteronomic lawyers; the teaching about God and his relations with his chosen people which the nation's laws are made to exemplify. We must remember that these laws would be very familiar to the people; justice was administered in the most public place in any city, and the laws are often cast in forms which are easy to remember and quote—short pithy sentences and successive clauses with exactly the same number of words in them, or which end with the same formal phrase. Whether they could read or not the ordinary Hebrews standing and watching the village elders hearing their neighbour's case at the village gate would certainly know what the Law was, and after the elders had got the facts of the case straight to the best of their ability, they would certainly know if they quoted the Law wrongly. There might be plenty of argument and contradictory witnesses about whether or not the local moneylender had gone into old Benjamin the sheepshearer's house to collect the clothes Benjamin had put up as surety for the loan, but there would be no argument or contradiction about what the Law said about it; anyone standing round would be able to quote it pat:

When you make your neighbour a loan of any sort, you shall not go into his house to fetch his pledge. You shall stand outside, and the man to whom you make the loan shall bring the pledge out to you.[1]

And everyone around knew that the Law forbade you to go over your field twice when you harvested the crop; you took all you could find and cut and carry of your crop and if you overlooked anything it was to be left for the landless foreigner living in your village, and for the orphans and widows. That was only fair, and everyone knew it. Everyone knew the Law, and *by this very fact* the new reasons added by the lawyers would stand out in the sharpest possible contrast; the new motives for obeying the Law would make an immediate impact. The conjunction of familiar and unfamiliar would drive home the new teaching with a force it could never have had if it had been presented alone; and, moreover, this new teaching was presented in its application to everyday life, not as a vague and abstract ideal without much obvious relevance:

When you beat your olive trees, you shall not go over the branches again: it shall be for the stranger, the fatherless, and for the widow. When you gather the grapes of your vineyard, you shall not glean it afterwards: it shall be for

[1] Deut. 24.10.

the stranger, the fatherless, and for the widow.[1]
And you shall remember that you were a slave
in the land of Egypt, (and the Lord your God
redeemed you from there): *therefore* I command
you to do this.[2]

They were God's chosen, and he made his choice
known to them, and his compassion for them, by
rescuing them from their slavery; so now they
were to show that same compassion to their help-
less neighbours; they were to turn their village
customs into signs pointing to the character of the
God whom they worshipped, expressions of his
steadfast love for his people. They would be act-
ing as God acted when he rescued them from
Egypt, and that same redeeming power would be
at work in their village life. It is a vision of God
which informs and irradiates the Law; the Law
is not changed: it is transfigured.

The major achievement, which overshadows
all else, was that of putting the nation's law into
the context of the escape from Egypt. The most
important aspect of Moses' work was to show
the people that their release from Egypt and their
escape from the Egyptian army and their survival
on the journey to Canaan was no accident but was
all the work of their God, Yahweh. All these
things are too hard for man to achieve and so
they show the power of God; they show that it is

[1] Deut. 24.20–21.
[2] Deut. 24.22, adding the extra phrase from Deut. 24.18.

his hand which is achieving it all. This, the very centre of Moses' work, the lawyers picked up again and made the key to the solution of the nation's problems. If the people would only again acknowledge that power of God, and return to its protection, and make it the motive power in their daily lives, then there was still a chance that the nation would survive and be brought back to health again. They had to take God's will and make it effective in their midst.

The nation's code of laws is given the escape from Egypt as its setting, and this is mainly done in the introductory passages, as we might expect. Those passages, 4.44–8.20 and 10.12–11.25, depict the Hebrews at the holy mountain, on their way from Egypt to Canaan, overawed by the revelation of the majesty and powers of God:

> Behold, the Lord our God has shown us his glory and his greatness, and we have heard his voice out of the midst of the fire: we have this day seen God speak with man, and man still live.[1]

But more than that, they also saw, said the lawyers, that they must keep the details of this God's will as it is expressed in testimonies (i.e., divine revelations of law), statues (that is decrees promulgated in writing), and judgements (the precedents established over the years in the day-to-

[1] Deut. 5.24.

day decisions about cases before the courts). And the ground of this obedience, the meaning of it, lay back in the deliverance God worked for them from Egypt and the continued acknowledgement of the sovereign authority of that power:

> When your son asks you in time to come, What is the meaning of the testimonies and the statutes and the judgements, which the Lord our God has commanded you? then you shall say to your son, We were Pharaoh's slaves in Egypt, and the Lord brought us out of Egypt with a mighty hand; and the Lord showed signs and wonders, great and grievous, against Egypt, and against Pharaoh, and all his household, before our eyes: and he brought us out from there, that he might bring us in, to give us the land which he swore to give to our fathers. And the Lord commanded us to do all these statutes, to fear the Lord our God, for our good always, that he might preserve us alive, as at this day. And it shall be righteousness for us, if we are careful to do all this commandment before the Lord our God, as he has commanded us.[1]

God was still concerned for his people, as he was concerned for them when they were in Egypt, but his presence in their midst was also the presence of *righteous* power. If that presence was

[1] Deut. 6.20–25.

to be a blessing to the people they, too, must be righteous. So it is at the very beginning of the introduction that the Decalogue, Ten Commandments, was given first of all so that it might set the pattern for the rest of the Law.[1] All the rest of the nation's law, in all its detail, was now to be seen as the expansion and detailed application of that primary law, the direct consequence of God's presence amongst them. Particularly is this true for all practices which acknowledge the existence of any gods other than Yahweh. All foreign worship must be ruthlessly stamped out, especially the hideous human sacrifices:

> Take heed that you be not ensnared to follow them, ... and that you do not inquire about their gods, saying, How did these nations serve their gods?—that I may do likewise. You shall not do so to the Lord your God; for every abominable thing which the Lord hates they have done for their gods; for they even burn their sons and their daughters in the fire to their gods.[2]

Any prophet who supported or encouraged foreign worship was to be executed,[3] even if he could perform miracles, and any of the ordinary people who continued to meddle with it were to

[1] Deut. 5.6–21.
[2] Deut. 12.30f.
[3] Deut. 13.1–5.

be killed if it was satisfactorily proved against them:

> If there is found among you . . . a man or woman who . . . has gone and served other gods and worshipped them, or the sun or the moon or any of the host of heaven . . . then you shall bring forth to your gates that man or woman who has done this evil thing, and you shall stone that man or woman to death with stones.[1]

It is this reason also which lies behind the prohibition of marriage with foreigners, for it is only natural that the alien would bring in his or her own native worship.

But in any case the lawyers did not expose this stamping out of foreign religious practices to the danger of lack of supervision. Clearly they were confident that with royal support there would be little difficulty in cleaning up Jerusalem and controlling the worship in the Temple. The danger lay with all the local sanctuaries scattered throughout the country, each with its local priests and loyalties, and each already deeply associated with the fertility cults. It would be an enormous task to supervise all of them, so a drastic solution to the problem was proposed. Henceforth there must be no more sacrifice at any of the local shrines. Only at the Temple in Jerusalem could there be sacrifice and any who wished to sacrifice must journey

[1] Deut. 17.2–7.

to Jerusalem to do so. Since all males had to be present at the sacrifices at least three times in the year at the great harvest feasts it would be possible to control the main religious activities of the whole population, and also make sure that the Jerusalem standards of worship were known throughout the country. And all this is quite apart from all the extraordinary sacrifices and vows in which every family would be involved at some time in the year: firstborn sons and the first lambs and calves, and tithes and a multitude of reasons and occasions when a sacrifice had to be offered. All would involve travelling up to Jerusalem. The lawyers were taking no chances. This Law of the Central Sanctuary occurs a number of times throughout the work, in close association with the command to destroy the altars of the foreign gods in the local sanctuaries. For only in Jerusalem was that place to be found where the Lord had chosen to put his name.

As we might expect, all this was supported by the conception of reward and punishment. If God was pleased with his people through their obedience it was only natural that they would be prosperous; if he was displeased with them it was only natural that their crops would suffer: for was he not the Lord of the harvest, the God of the corn and the wine and the oil? Above all, their very possession of the land depended on this obedience, and if they disobeyed they would be removed from it. This may seem a peculiar threat to us, but let us remember that these people had seen this happen to their brethren and neighbours in the northern kingdom. Only a matter of twenty or thirty years before they had seen the Assyrians deport the population of Israel wholesale and bring other people in. No greater threat could have been made; it would be the one thing everyone deeply feared.

The lawyers took the teaching of the eighth-century Prophets and turned it into legislation. Or rather, they took the country's traditional and familiar legislation and used it as a vehicle to carry the Prophets' teaching into the lives of the people. Yet there is also a remarkable difference and it is mainly a difference in tone. I should not have said that there was much laughter about the eighth-century Prophets. Amos and Hosea and Isaiah were too caught up in the agony of their people's apostasy for them to teach much about laughter; they were too aware of the impending doom brooding over the nation, and how much the people deserved it. Truly there is much of mercy and hope and even of joy in Hosea and Isaiah; but it is a hope cast in the distant future, a joy which can only be realized after deep suffering and purging and judgement which will leave only a remnant of the people to enjoy it. In Deuteronomy, on the other hand, there is a phrase which keeps recurring: "You shall rejoice":

> There you shall eat before the Lord your God,
> and you shall rejoice in all that you undertake,
> you and your households, in which the Lord
> your God has blessed you.[1]

And the lawyer means it for now. "You shall
rejoice in all that you undertake." Here and now.
The Hebrew word means "gladness, mirth,
laughter":

> They joy before thee as with joy in harvest, as
> men rejoice when they divide the spoil.[2]

Those are Isaiah's words, but describing the far
distant messianic age. For Deuteronomy this
same deeply satisfied joy could be found now in
the simple, everyday, ordinary things of life:

> The Lord your God will bless you in all your
> produce, and in all the work of your hands,
> so that you will be altogether joyful.[3]

"You will be altogether joyful." It is that more
than anything I would like to leave with you of
Deuteronomy; the deep and contented and altogether natural laughter of a people at peace and
at home with their God in their everyday lives.
It lies at the heart of the lawyers' vision.

There was no hope of any of this being put into
practical effect while Manasseh was alive, no

[1] Deut. 12.7.
[2] Isa. 9.3
[3] Deut. 16.15.

hope of his promulgating this book as law for his people, so the lawyers worked at it secretly. But after his death it was tried by the king who came next but one to the throne. And one of the young men alive in Judah at the time, the son of a country priest living just outside Jerusalem, was named Jeremiah.

NOTE: KEY TEXTS IN DEUTERONOMY

	The book found in 621:
Deut. 4.44–8.20; 10.12–11.25	Introduction
chs. 12–26	The laws
chs. 28–9.1	Conclusion
2 Kings 21–3.30	Historical background
6.13,20–5; 7.8,18; 8.2–5,14–18; 10.19–22; 11.2–7; 13.5,17–18; 15.15,18; 16.1–8; 17.16; 20.1; 23.4; 24.9,18,22; 25.17; 26.8	The escape from Egypt
5.22–6; 7.21; 8.19–20; 10.14,17	Majesty of God
5.2–3; 7.8,12; 8.18; 17.3	The Covenant
6.14–15; 7.1–16,25–6; 8.19; 11.16–17; 12.3,29–31; 13.1–5; 16.21–2; 17.2–7; 18.9–14; 20.16–18; 28.14	Destruction of foreign worship

12.5–7,11–14,17–18,26–7; 14.23–6; 15.20; 16.2–17; 17.8–10; 18.6–8; 23.17–18; 26.1–11	The Central Sanctuary
5.33; 6.2–3,15; 7.9–15; 8.1–20; 11.8–17,21–5; 12.25–8; 13.17; 14.24–9; 15.10; 16.20; 19.13; 22.6–7; 25.15; 26.15; 28	Rewards and punishments
14.2,21; 23.14; 24.4; 26.15–19; 28.9	Holy people
15.1–11,14; 16.18–20; 19.1–13,14–20; 20.5–8; 21.10–14; 22.1–4; 23.15–16, 19–20,24–5; 24.5–6,10–22; 25.1–4,13–15,26.12	Social laws
7.9,12	"Steadfast love"
28.25–57	Foreign enemies as God's tools
5.6–21	The Decalogue, the type of all law

The traditional laws and quasi-legal material used by the Deuteronomic lawyers:

1. The Canaanite "Ritual Decalogue": Exod. 22.29–30; 23.12,15–19; 34.10–26; Deut. 5.12–15; 14.21–22; 15.19–23; 16.3–8,9–16; 18.4; 26.1–11. (The Deuteronomy references are mainly expansions.)

2. The Old Canaanite Civil Code: Deut. 15.12–18; 21.15–23; 22.6–8,13–29; 23.21–5; 24.1–4,10–12,19; 25.1–3. Also 19.16–20; 24.7.

3. The *Lex Talionis*: "An eye for an eye": 19.21
4. Cultic obligations: 16.21–17.1
5. Instructions for judges: 16.19
6. Unnatural combinations: 22.5,9–11
7. Qualifications for membership of the Full Assembly 22.30–23.3,7
8. Old cultic usages:
   21.1–9:   Cleansing after murder where the murderer is not discovered
   26.1–11:   Ritual for offering first-fruits
   20.1–9:   Seventh-century adaptation of an old army regulation
9. Recent traditions:
   13.1–5:   True and false prophets
   13.6–18:   People who return to idolatry
   17.14–20: The king
   18.9–22:   Canaanite divination; the mediating prophet
   19.1–13:   Cities of refuge

There are certainly other blocks of traditional material used or adapted by the Deuteronomic lawyers, but the above are the ones which may be separated with some confidence.

6

JEREMIAH: THE EARLY YEARS

THE period which we shall be considering in this chapter is one of the most eventful in the whole history of the ancient world. During it the apparently impregnable and all-powerful empire of Assyria was battered to pieces and destroyed by the upsurge of Babylon. Egypt snatched at the opportunity and marched right through into Mesopotamia with the Pharaoh at her head, and in her turn was also defeated and driven back into her home country. Within the space of little more than a handful of years the whole of the Near East exploded and settled down again into a different pattern of power. And it is just at this time that Jeremiah, as a young man, started his ministry. That ministry was going to stretch over forty years and only end when Jerusalem had been destroyed and the country laid waste and the people carried off into slavery in Babylon.

The inspiration and driving power which carved out a great empire for Assyria and held it in a ruthless grip was essentially a personal power.

The personal drive and ruthless rule of a series of five outstanding soldier kings made and maintained Assyrian greatness. When that central drive and direction failed the whole great empire collapsed with surprising speed. The first cracks in the structure begin to show about the middle of the seventh century, when the king's brother led a rebellion. The king, Ashurbanipal, crushed it, but his control became increasingly uncertain, and it is significant that the rebellious brother was at the time governor of the provincial city of Babylon. Perhaps Ashurbanipal was not sufficiently interested in the military strength by which alone the Empire was held together: he is famous more for his great library than for any conquests. There is a charming relief in the British Museum of Ashurbanipal and his queen feasting in a garden, surrounded by musicians and servants. But although there is no sign of guards and the king himself is unarmed, yet the head of an executed enemy is hanging in a nearby tree, so perhaps Ashurbanipal was not as soft as the historians make him out to be.

The chaos really broke out when first one son and then another occupied the throne after Ashurbanipal's death. Sixty years earlier an Assyrian king had given Babylon, the town and district near the Persian gulf, the full Assyrian colonial treatment: destruction and deportation. A few years later another Assyrian king rebuilt it and populated it again. But this time the colonial policy did not work. At Ashurbanipal's death the Babylonians rose again and soon the whole of the north-east of Mesopotamia was aflame with revolt and an army was on the very point of capturing Nineveh itself, the capital of the Empire.

Only one thing saved Nineveh, and that only for a few brief years. With the weakening of the Assyrian power and the fighting within the heart of the Empire, the vital watch over the mountain passes behind Assyria could no longer be maintained. The guards were withdrawn as troops were recalled to try and save Nineveh itself, and through the passes flooded the barbarian hordes which only Assyrian power had kept in check. These people were called Scythians, and their original home lay deep in what is now Russia, in the vast unknown tracts beyond the Black Sea and the Caucasus. Once through the mountain passes they fanned out over the whole Mesopotamian area with no particular plan or co-ordination, massacring, and laying waste whatever district they passed through. At one stage they even reached the frontiers of Egypt, but they did not penetrate into the land. The fall of Nineveh was staved off for another fourteen years as the threatening Babylonians found that they were themselves in danger of being overwhelmed by the ravaging Scythians.

It is just at this time that Jeremiah first made

his presence known. Ironically, the chaos and fighting at the heart of Assyria brought a period of peace to Judah and a blessed release from interference. As the military power of the Empire was withdrawn to protect its very heart, so the outlying provinces and subject kingdoms found the burden of Assyrian occupation lifted; amongst those who experienced relief was Judah. The long and spiritually desolate reign of Manasseh had at last ended. During its fifty-five years Jerusalem had seen human sacrifice in which men had followed the king's example and burned their children. His surviving son had followed his father's practices during the two years he was on the throne, and then he was assassinated in a palace intrigue. It would be pleasant to be able to say that the people had risen against him and his debased religion, in defence of Yahweh their God, but there is no evidence for this. Indeed, if anything, the way the people hunted down and killed all who had been concerned in the revolt rather points away from this. His son Josiah succeeded him at the age of eight and reigned for thirty-one years. It is a reign to remember, for it was by Josiah's initiative and under his direction that there was a last brief and glorious flowering of Judah and a thorough attempt to undo the long tragic years of desertion and disobedience. Possibly the people were already too far gone for any reform to be fully effective, in

5

any case Josiah was still only in his thirties when he fell at the head of his army, and his reform died with him. But all that lies in the future.

Josiah was just twenty when Jeremiah's voice was first heard, and the prophet himself must have been about the same age. For some reasons the Scythians had left Judah alone, but all the country to the north had already suffered from their pillaging and Jeremiah saw clearly the threat hanging over the kingdom. It was against the background of this threat that he first became aware of his prophetic call.

> The word of the Lord came to me saying, Before I formed you in the womb I knew you, and before you were born I consecrated you; I appointed you a prophet to the nations.[1]

From the very beginning Jeremiah was deeply conscious that his prophetic vocation was no passing or temporary thing, but part of the far-reaching plan by which God was working out his people's redemption. This consciousness that everything is under God's control was the spring from which Jeremiah's incredible patience flowed, and which enabled him to see God's plan being worked out even when the Babylonians were setting fire to Jerusalem and driving the people away in slave gangs. But his first reaction was to pro-

[1] Jer. 1.4f.

test that he was too young for such heavy responsibility:

> Then I said, Ah, Lord God! Behold, I do not know how to speak, for I am only a youth. But the Lord said to me, Do not say, I am only a youth; for to all to whom I send you you shall go, and whatever I command you you shall speak. Be not afraid of them, for I am with you to deliver you, says the Lord.[1]

Later Jeremiah would indeed need that reassurance. With an echo of Isaiah's experience of the angel touching his lips, the passage continues:

> Then the Lord put forth his hand and touched my mouth; and the Lord said to me, Behold, I have put my words in your mouth. See, I have set you this day over nations and over kingdoms, to pluck up and break down, to destroy and to overthrow, to build and to plant.[2]

It is not surprising that the youth, possibly still only in his teens, protested that he was too young for such a task. So he was given a sign to reassure him of God's protection, a sign with one of those puns which the Prophets found so significant. He saw the branch of an almond tree; perhaps there was an almond tree growing in the place where he experienced the presence and call of God. The Hebrew for an almond is *shaqudh*, the same sound as *shoqedh*, which means "watching".

[1] Jer. 1.6–8.
[2] Jer. 1.9–10.

> And the word of the Lord came to me, saying, Jeremiah, what do you see? and I said, I see a branch of an almond. Then the Lord said to me, You have seen well, for I am watching over my word to perform it.[1]

And the Hebrew uses the pronoun emphatically here: *I* am watching. At no time in his ministry would this most lonely of all the prophets ever be alone, for God would be watching and directing and protecting him.

Although Josiah had been on the throne of Judah for twelve years at this time he was still only twenty years old at the most. To be sure he had not sunk into the religious degradation of his grandfather and father, but nor had he made any attempt to undo their sixty years of faithlessness. It would be several years yet before he launched the great reform by which his reign is remembered. Meanwhile the Scythian scourge hung over the kingdom and in it Jeremiah saw the fulfilment of his vocation. Here lay the reason God had called him: to call the people to repentance; to call them to undo the long years of faithlessness and return to Yahweh their God while there was still time. In the barbarian menace Jeremiah saw the hand of God, his patience finally exhausted, come to punish his chosen ones for deserting him:

> The word of the Lord came to me a second

[1] Jer. 1.11–12.

time, saying, what do you see? And I said,
I see a boiling pot, facing away from the north.
Then the Lord said to me, Out of the north
evil shall break forth upon all the inhabitants
of the land. For, lo, I am calling all the tribes
of the kingdoms of the north, says the Lord. . . .
And I will utter my judgements against [Judah
and Jerusalem], for all their wickedness in for-
saking me; they have burned incense to other
gods, and worshipped the works of their own
hands.[1]

The Scythians were poised over the land like a
great cauldron filled and boiling and slowly tilting
towards them, about to pour out its scalding contents over them.

In the intensity of his awareness of the danger,
and his consciousness that the people could no
longer have any claim on Yahweh's protection,
Jeremiah wrote as if the dreaded hordes were
already amongst them:

At the noise of horseman and archer
    every city takes flight;
they enter thickets; they climb among rocks;
    all the cities are forsaken,
    and no man dwells in them.[2]

O my pain, my pain!
O walls of my heart!

[1] Jer. 1.13–16.
[2] Jer. 4.29.

My heart is beating wildly;
  I cannot keep silent;
for I hear the sound of the trumpet,
  the alarm of war.
Disaster follows hard on disaster,
  the whole land is laid waste.[1]

Yet Jerusalem seemed to go on with business as usual; few showed any sign of realizing the danger. Even now they trusted in their empty worship, in the gods of their fertility rites. But they would find that they were powerless to help:

And you, O desolate one,
  what do you mean that you dress in scarlet,
    that you deck yourself with ornaments of
      gold,
    that you enlarge your eyes with paint?
In vain you beautify yourself.
  Your lovers despise you;
    they seek your life.[2]

O Jerusalem, wash your heart from wickedness,
  that you may be saved.
How long shall your evil thoughts lodge within
  you?[3]

But they escaped. The threatened inundation never came, and as the danger receded the king's

[1] Jer. 4.19ff.
[2] Jer. 4.30.
[3] Jer. 4.14.

thoughts turned to the long-needed repairs to the Temple buildings.

For some time it must have been clear that extensive repairs were needed in the great complex of buildings in the heart of Jerusalem which comprised the Temple. For some time the doorkeepers had been collecting money, from all who passed through the Temple gates, to meet the costs of repairs, and now the king commanded that this money be given to the master workmen who had the oversight of the fabric, so that they could hire masons and carpenters and buy materials and get the work started. In the account of all this in 2 Kings (4 Kings) there is one charming verse which opens a window into the attitude of those concerned, the deep trust they had one for another:

> But no accounting shall be asked from them for the money which is delivered into their hand, says the king, For they deal honestly.[1]

Tucked into a crack in one of the walls, where it would be found when the masons started their repairs, was a scroll. When unrolled it would be about fifteen feet long by about ten inches broad: rolled up it was quite bulky and not likely to be overlooked easily. Written on it was a codification of the nation's laws with an explanatory commentary. Clearly at a glance whoever had made

[1] 2 Kings 22.7. (4 Kings 22.7.)

the arrangement and written the commentary had been fired with a breathtaking vision of the universal tenderness and majesty and love and compassion of Yahweh the God of the Hebrews, and had also passionately longed for the people to be at peace with God and restored again to the deep joy which that peace brings. The book written on the scroll was what we now know as Deuteronomy. Since it was written in secret sometime during the long, slow fifty-five years of Manasseh's reign, as the nation sank deeper and deeper into its degenerate and sensual and double-minded religious confusion, there could have been no hope at the time of it finding practical expression. It had to wait until a sympathetic king was prepared to give it royal support and, if necessary, back the reform with force. It had to wait until Manasseh's death.

It would be nice to think that the book lay in some crevice of the Temple walls collecting dust through the years until Josiah decided to have the walls repaired, but it is unlikely that the reform lawyers left it so much to chance. Much more probably it was kept secretly and closely, and passed down the years through faithful keepers until the time was ripe and a king arose who would take it seriously. Whoever had charge of it at the time (and who more likely than Hilkiah the High Priest in Jerusalem?), judged that the moment had arrived when Josiah reached the age of twenty-five. Already he had reigned for eighteen years, and for the last seven of those, from the age of eighteen, he would be in effective control himself and free from the direction of regents. There would have been ample time to see how he shaped and where his sympathies lay. As the work started on the Temple walls, Hilkiah came to the king's secretary with the news that he had found the Book of the Law in the house of the Lord. Shaphan took it and read it to the King.

The effect on the king must have surpassed Hilkiah's wildest hopes:

> And when the king heard the words of the book of the law, he rent his clothes. And the king commanded Hilkiah the priest, and Ahikam the son of Shaphan, and Achbor the son of Micaiah, and Shaphan the secretary, and Asaiah the king's servant, saying, Go, inquire of the Lord for me, and for the people, and for all Judah, concerning the words of this book that has been found; for great is the wrath of the Lord that is kindled against us, because our fathers have not obeyed the words of this book, to do all that is written concerning us.[1]

Although for long before Josiah's day the king's court had been the centre of religious corruption, there must have been people in Judah, and many of them influential, who regretted the nation's degradation and longed for the opportunity of

[1] 2 Kings 22.11–13 (4 Kings).

seeing the Prophets' teachings put into practice and the nation's religion purified. The reform initiated by the king was both extensive and drastic, and could only have been carried through with substantial support amongst the people.

In the field of international power, too, this was the moment of opportunity. Assyrian control had gone with the Assyrian troops. The Assyrian garrisons had been withdrawn for the defence of Nineveh. The Assyrian troops had enforced religious control as well as political, and before we judge Manasseh and his son Amon, Josiah's father, too harshly, we must remember that Assyria would have read treason into any attempt to purge Judah of the Assyrian religion. Be that as it may, now was the chance, and directed and encouraged by Hilkiah, the High Priest, and the whole prophetic party, Josiah grasped it firmly.

The purpose of the reform was to restore the people's loyalty to Yahweh their God and stamp out of their lives and worship all that was unworthy of him. The lawyers who translated this vision into practical details saw clearly that they had no chance of success unless there was firm direction and control. The reform must have teeth, or it would be as ineffective in practice as had been the teachings of the Prophets: fine ideals and true, but without effect in the people's daily lives. And if there was to be firm direction and control there had to be centralization, and that meant Jerusalem. All the nation's worship, and in particular the great festivals when all males must attend the sacrifices, must be centred on Jerusalem and the Temple, the Royal Chapel. So to the Temple in Jerusalem the king summoned the entire population of Jerusalem and also the elders, the magistrates and local men of influence from every town and village throughout the country. To this great gathering the king read the newly discovered Book of the Law, and together with them he then solemnly renewed the Covenant and dedicated the nation afresh to the service of their God, Yahweh, and obedience to his will:

> Then the king sent, and all the elders of Judah and Jerusalem were gathered to him. And the king went up to the house of the Lord, and with him all the men of Judah and all the inhabitants of Jerusalem, and the priests and the prophets, all the people, both small and great; and he read in their hearing all the words of the book of the covenant which had been found in the house of the Lord. And the king stood by the pillar and made a covenant before the Lord, to walk after the Lord and to keep his commandments and his testimonies and his statutes, with all his heart and all his soul, to perform the words of this covenant that were written in this book; and all the people joined in the covenant.[1]

[1] 2 Kings 23.1–3. (4 Kings 23.1–3.)

The work of clearing the Temple of all foreign worship began immediately. The altars and sacred vessels used in the fertility cults were broken down and the pieces burned and the ashes carried right out of the country. The ghastly shrine Topheth in the deep Valley of Hinnom just outside the south wall of the city was ceremonially defiled, "that no one might burn his son or his daughter as an offering to Molech",[1] and the whole rabble of strange priests and sacred prostitutes and diviners and astrologers and necromancers were driven from the city.

When the purification of Jerusalem was complete the royal commissioners, escorted by soldiers, worked their way through the country districts, destroying the local shrines and forbidding the country priests to sacrifice and defiling the high places and cutting down the sacred groves of the fertility cults. The young king himself rode north into what had once been the northern kingdom of Israel before the Assyrians had destroyed and repopulated it and turned it into an Assyrian province. Now the Assyrian soldiers had been withdrawn and Josiah thrust through the country enforcing his reform on the people and destroying their shrines. He must have met with some resistance here, for some of the local priests lost their lives in the process:

[1] 2 Kings 23.10. (4 Kings 23.10)

> And all the shrines also of the high places that were in the cities of Samaria, which kings of Israel had made, provoking the Lord to anger, Josiah removed; . . . And he slew all the priests of the high places who were there, upon the altars, and burned the bones of men upon them. Then he returned to Jerusalem.[1]

It says much for Josiah's control of the country, and also for the desire for reform there must have been amongst the people, that the opposition was not greater. For the pagan priests would not be the only ones offended. Throughout the country there were also faithful priests of Yahweh ministering to their districts at the village shrines, the priests of the country parishes. At a stroke their local position was destroyed, for no longer could they officiate at their people's sacrifices. Together with their parishioners they, too, must travel to Jerusalem for every major act of worship. Josiah and the Jerusalem priests at the centre of the new reform encouraged them to take their turn in officiating at the Temple services, but at least the greater part of these country priests refused the offer. They stayed in the country, and no doubt a good deal of illegal sacrificing continued on the quiet. All this is of importance to us, for it was to one of these families of country priests, living in the village of

[1] 2 Kings 23.19f. (4 Kings 23.19f.)

Anathoth, that Jeremiah belonged. His father was the village priest.

Anathoth was only about five miles out of Jerusalem. When the king's commissioners with their armed escort rode out into the country to enforce the reform, Anathoth would be one of the first places reached. As son of the parish priest Jeremiah would be there when the king's men pulled down the village shrine and broke up the altar at which his father and a long line of ancestors had sacrificed to Yahweh. How did Jeremiah respond to all this?

> The word that came to Jeremiah from the Lord: Hear the words of this covenant, and speak to the men of Judah and the inhabitants of Jerusalem. . . . Proclaim all these words in the cities of Judah, and in the streets of Jerusalem: hear the words of this covenant and do them. For I solemnly warned your fathers when I brought them up out of the land of Egypt, warning them persistently, even to this day, saying, Obey my voice.[1]

"Speak to the men of Judah and the inhabitants of Jerusalem." Jeremiah's response to the reform was to support it publicly and enthusiastically, to journey through the capital and the country districts urging the people to accept the reform in all its details. This was their chance, their oppor-

[1] Jer. 11.1f,6f.

tunity to undo the long years of disobedience.
Legally speaking, God had every right to declare
the Covenant void because the people had broken
their side of the agreement, but he had again
given them time for reform. They must use it.

His family must have been dismayed, for their
reaction was violent. At first Jeremiah did not
realize that their anger was directed against himself, that there were plots in his own village to
silence him:

> I was like a gentle lamb led to the slaughter.
> I did not know it was against me they devised
> schemes, saying,
> Let us destroy the tree with its fruit,
>   let us cut him off from the land of the living,
>   that his name be remembered no more.[1]

His first act on hearing that they were planning to
stop his prophesying was to turn on his village
and warn them furiously of the punishment they
might expect for the sacrilege of daring to silence
a prophet:

> Thus says the Lord concerning the men of
> Anathoth, who seek your life, and say, Do not
> prophesy in the name of the Lord, or you will
> die by our hand—therefore thus says the Lord
> of hosts: Behold I will punish them; the young
> men shall die by the sword; their sons and their

[1] Jer. 11.19.

daughters shall die by famine; and none of them shall be left.[1]

Later, when a king less pious had turned against him, and the princes of the king's court were howling for his blood, Jeremiah looked back wistfully on this time when he first experienced opposition. He looked back and reflected how mild was this opposition of his family and friends compared with all that was to come. Their menace could be avoided as easily as a good sprinter outpaces those chasing him; the later menace would be like trying to outpace horses. Then he had been in clear safety compared with the hidden jungle of the forces which tried to silence him later in his life:

> If you have raced with men on foot, and they have wearied you, how will you compete with horses?
> And if in a safe land you fall down, how will you do in the jungle of Jordan?[2]

But at the moment when he first realized that he had to turn away from his home and his own relatives and the security into which he was born, he did so sadly and bitterly:

> I have forsaken my house, I have abandoned my heritage,
> I have given the beloved of my soul into the hands of her enemies.

[1] Jer. 11.21–3.
[2] Jer. 12.5.

My heritage has become to me like a lion in
    the forest,
  she has lifted up her voice against me;
  therefore I hate her.
Is my heritage to me like a speckled bird of
    prey?
Are the birds of prey against her round about?
Go, assemble all the wild beasts;
  bring them to devour.[1]

It would have been easier to bear if he could
have felt confident about the reform itself, but as
the nation settled down to the new way of life his
confidence in it ebbed away. In one way the reform was all too successful: it established the
authority of Jerusalem once and for all and the
Temple as the place of the presence of God. Their
God was there, dwelling invisibly but with un-
questioned certainty in the Temple, enthroned in
the dark mystery of the Holy of Holies. But this
belief produced in the people a growing and
deadly complacency. God was enthroned in their
midst; nothing could happen to them; they were
secure. For most of the people the heart of the
lawyers' vision was lost. The ideal at the heart of
Deuteronomy, that their daily lives should be
expressions of their love for Yahweh their God,
quietly faded away. Slowly the people drifted
back to their old ways; even the old ways of worship, the foreign idols, crept back here and there

[1] Jer. 12.7–9.

in the land. To his dismay Jeremiah saw the time
going by and the chance of salvation being lost:
"The harvest is past, and we are not saved":

> My grief is beyond healing, my heart is sick
> with me.
> Hark, the cry of the daughter of my people
> from the length and breadth of the land:
> "Is the Lord not in Zion?
> Is her King not in her?"
> Why have they provoked me to anger with
> their graven images, and with their foreign
> idols?
> The harvest is past, the summer is ended, and
> we are not saved.
> For the wound of the daughter of my people
> is my heart wounded,
> I mourn, and dismay has taken hold on me.[1]

The summer indeed was ended, and far sooner
than anyone dreamed of. By the year 609, the
Assyrians had been fighting in defence of their
own homeland for sixteen years. First the great
provincial fortresses fell to the Babylonians, and
then Nineveh itself was taken and destroyed.
Only the remote north-west part of the great
Empire was still under Assyrian control. At this
stage Egypt saw her opportunity. Hoping that
both Assyrians and Babylonians would be too
weakened by the long war to offer any effective

[1] Jer. 8.18–22.

resistance, Pharaoh Neco with a powerful Egyptian army moved north to Mesopotamia to see what Egypt could capture from the wreckage. He marched his army up the coast road, avoiding Jerusalem, but Josiah felt that he should oppose his passage. Whether he thought Judah and his army stronger than it was, or whether he too, like his people, thought that the presence of God in the Temple would guarantee success, there is no knowing. The Judaean army marched out on its suicidal mission with King Josiah at its head. They met the Egyptians at Megiddo and were inevitably defeated, and although Josiah's servants managed to get the mortally wounded king out of the battle, he died before they reached Jerusalem again. With his death the summer ended, and the people had not been saved. The nation sank into paralysed fear.

Why do we sit still?
Gather together, let us go into the fortified
    cities and perish there;
For the Lord our God has doomed us to
    perish. . . .
We looked for peace, but no good came, for a
    time of healing, but behold, terror.[1]

[1] Jer. 8.14f.

JEREMIAH: THE FALL OF JERUSALEM

WITH King Josiah's death at Megiddo in 609 the brief summer of Hebrew hope ended; the time of opportunity had passed. Very few of the people realized it. City merchant, country peasant, priest of the Temple at Jerusalem or nobleman at court—almost all thought that the nation had been purged and rededicated, cleansed and renewed and restored to the faithful service of Yahweh their God. His presence in the Temple, throned between the great cherubim in the secrecy of the Holy of Holies, seated in invisible majesty on the Ark, would protect them from any drastic harm, any final catastrophe. Josiah's death in battle shook their complacency, but it was very far from destroying it.

While the body of the king was being carried back to Jerusalem the victorious Egyptian army moved on north. Their march had barely been interrupted by Josiah's suicidal gesture, and they pushed on to their true objective, the wreck of the Assyrian homeland. Josiah's son Jehoahaz

took over the government and the country
settled down to its old life. But not for long. Her
few years of political independence were over.
Pharaoh Neco carried the Egyptian army across
the great River Euphrates, ostensibly to help the
last Assyrian king still holding out there with the
remains of the army he had managed to save
from the fall of his capital, Nineveh. There is no
clear account of what happened. Perhaps the
Egyptians found the Babylonians stronger than
they expected and far from exhausted by the long
war with Assyria. At any rate, after some confused fighting the Pharaoh took his army back
across the Euphrates again and settled down to
organize Palestine and Syria. These, in any case,
were his most valuable prize, for they were
nearest Egypt and must be his first line of defence
against any northern threat.

Judah found itself the first place to be
organized. Jehoahaz the king was peremptorily
summoned to the Egyptian army headquarters
north of Damascus. There he was deposed and
imprisoned. His only sight of Judah again was to
be when he passed down the coast road under
Egyptian guard on his way to captivity and death
in Egypt. His brief reign was ended before the
people had finished mourning for his father
Josiah:

> Weep not for him who is dead, nor bemoan
> him;

But weep bitterly for him who goes away,
    for he shall return no more
    to see his native land.[1]

Already Jeremiah was beginning to see what this meant for the nation. Another of Josiah's sons, Jehoiakim, was put on the throne as Pharaoh's puppet, and under Egyptian direction a great fine was imposed on the country and everyone assessed for their share in paying it. Pharaoh meant his hand to be felt throughout the land. At a stroke the freedom which the fall of Assyria had brought faded away.

Jehoiakim was twenty-five when he so unexpectedly found himself king of Jerusalem, the same age as his father Josiah had been when he had initiated the great reform and renewed the Covenant with God and driven out the strange and foreign sects which for so long had defiled the country. But Jehoiakim was no second Josiah and under him what little of value remained of his father's reform sank out of sight. From now until the capture and then the destruction of Jerusalem twenty-two years later the history of these people was one of steady spiritual and political decline. The spiritual decline is to be measured by the relentless movement, official as well as popular, away from the reform whose spirit is so wonderfully expressed in the Book of

[1] Jer. 22.10.

Deuteronomy. The political decline is to be measured by the failure of successive kings to realize that their independence had gone. By a series of hopeless revolts the kings of Judah provoked the overwhelming power of Babylon, until Babylon saw clearly that she had no choice but to silence them. Every sign of patience or leniency shown by Babylon Judah interpreted as weakness, until finally Babylon solved her problem and did for Judah what Assyria had done for the northern kingdom, Israel, a hundred and thirty years earlier. Then Judah had appealed for Assyrian help in her struggle against Israel and Assyria had destroyed Judah's northern brethren and kinsfolk. Now Judah in her turn was to pay exactly the same penalty for exactly the same reason: revolt against the colonial power which controlled her.

But there was one man who faced the stark reality of the situation without any illusions, and who drew the only possible conclusions: Jeremiah. And it was not only the political situation he saw so clearly. His growing disquiet over the progress of the reform and his fears that its effects had only been superficial, reached certainty. Certain at last after his long years of comparative silence, he now spoke out clearly and publicly and uncompromisingly.

The key to the reform's practical effect on the people, as we have seen, lay in control over the popular religion, and that control was obtained by making Jerusalem's Temple the central and sole authority in all religious matters and the only place where the all-important sacrifices could be offered. As all people in the country were obliged to attend at least certain main sacrifices every year, the whole population were brought under the control of the Jerusalem priests. Perhaps if Josiah had lived he might have managed to make this central control a way of filling the nation with true devotion, he might have changed the people's hearts. But after his death his reform hardened into an empty religion of externals and superstition. It is this that Jeremiah saw and condemned as he looked at his nation dispassionately.

In the beginning of the reign of Jehoiakim the son of Josiah, king of Judah, this word came from the Lord, Thus says the Lord: Stand in the court of the Lord's house, and speak to all the cities of Judah which come to worship in the house of the Lord all the words that I command you to speak to them; do not hold back a word. . . . Thus says the Lord: If you will not listen to me, to walk in my law which I have set before you, and to heed the words of my servants the prophets whom I send to you urgently . . . then I will make this house like Shiloh, and I will make this city a curse for all the nations of the earth.[1]

[1] Jer. 26.1–6.

"I will make this house like Shiloh." All in the Temple court that day would know what those words meant. It was at Shiloh that Eli had been priest. Shiloh had been the great central sanctuary of the tribes when they first entered the promised land; it was there that the Ark had rested. And it was from Shiloh that the Ark was carried into battle against the Philistines in a last attempt to turn defeat into victory:

> Why has the Lord put us to rout today before the Philistines? Let us bring the ark of the covenant of the Lord here from Shiloh, that he may come among us and save us from the power of our enemies.[1]

But it did not work. The Ark, the place of Yahweh's presence, failed to hold back the Philistines. It was itself captured and Shiloh destroyed —as recent excavations on the site of the old sanctuary have proved. And now Jeremiah was holding this before the people as a warning. What God once did to Shiloh he would again do to this Temple in which they were worshipping. There was a deep and poignant undercurrent running in Jeremiah's words, a fittingness which made it appropriate that it should be he who spoke these words. For Jeremiah was himself descended from Eli the priest of Shiloh; his priestly family in Anathoth was descended from the only son of

[1] 1 Sam. 4.3. (1 Kings 4.3.)

Eli to survive the disaster. That disaster at Shiloh
had been caused by the faithlessness of his own
family and it was fitting that Jeremiah should
now rise to denounce the same faithlessness in the
priests and people of his day, and warn them that
the same fate would overtake them. One wonders
how many of the great crowd in the Temple court
realized that the heir of Shiloh's priest was speaking.

The immediate effect was a riot. Stirred up by
the priests and the official prophets, the worshipping congregation changed to an angry mob and
turned on Jeremiah to kill him. It was very nearly
the end of his ministry, but fortunately the court
heard the noise and the princes and elders, the
judiciary of Judah, assembled quickly to hear
the case. It is clear that there were two distinct
parties amongst the country's leaders. The priests
and prophets would tolerate no interference.
Jeremiah had threatened the holy Temple itself,
the throne of God, and he must die. But calmer
counsels prevailed. Some of the elders (and the
son of Shaphan was amongst them—that Shaphan
who had first read the newly discovered Deuteronomy to King Josiah)—some of the elders re-
minded the people that this was not the first time
a prophet had threatened Jerusalem. Their fathers
had heard the same denunciations from Micah
and they had listened to him with fear. They
warned the princes and people:

We are about to bring great evil upon ourselves.[1]

The people were convinced and Jeremiah escaped.
But the king revealed his character in the sequel.
Like a spoiled child who cannot bear to be
crossed, he vented his anger on another and
less fortunate prophet, Uriah. Uriah had also
spoken out against Jerusalem and its shallowness,
and then had fled to Egypt. Now Jehoiakim sent
armed men after him (being Egypt's puppet had
its advantages). They brought him under arrest to
Jerusalem and there Jehoiakim beheaded him.
The moderate party must learn their place.

But the lesson was lost on Jeremiah. All he
could see was the hypocrisy at the heart of the
people's religion. The Temple had been repaired
and the services were maintained with all the
care men can give to them. And at the same time
all the old injustices continued in the land. The
social and religious wrongs condemned by every
prophet from Amos were still being committed;
and committed, moreover, by the very people who
filled the Temple at the times of sacrifice; their
presence had turned the Temple into a thieves'
kitchen. There lay the real sacrilege:

Behold, you trust in deceptive words to no
avail. Will you steal, murder, commit adultery,
swear falsely, burn incense to Baal, and go after

[1] Jer. 26.19.

other gods that you have not known, and then
come and stand before me in this house, which
is called by my name, and say, We are
delivered!—only to go on doing these abomina-
tions? Has this house, which is called by my
name, become a den of robbers in your eyes?
Behold, I myself have seen it, says the Lord.[1]

The people had made the very Temple itself
the centre of their false and hollow religion. They
had all the externals, and none of the spirit of
their God. The Temple had become the mere
symbol of their complacency. They thought its
mere presence in their midst sufficient to prevent
any harm coming to the nation; they had forgotten
that first and foremost they would model their
lives on the pattern of their God; that they should
take the character he had revealed to them and
show it in all that they did. It was this that the
Deuteronomic lawyers had seen so clearly; this
that Josiah had tried to pour into his people by
force; and this one essential truth that Jeremiah
saw clearly was missing:

Do not trust in these deceptive words: This
is the temple of the Lord, the temple of the
Lord, the temple of the Lord. Thus says
the Lord of hosts, the God of Israel; Add
your burnt offerings to your sacrifices, and
eat the flesh. For in the day that I brought them

[1] Jer. 7.8–11.

out of the land of Egypt, I did not speak to your fathers or command them concerning burnt offerings and sacrifices. But this command I gave them, Obey my voice, and I will be your God, and you shall be my people; and walk in all the way that I command you, that it may be well with you.[1]

No-one listened to him. The king was hostile and the remnant of the reform party thought it best to stay silent.

But the time was running out quickly and the fast-moving international situation changed yet again and the new pattern began to show clearly. Babylon swept away the last traces of Assyrian resistance in 606 and was at last free to give Egypt her undivided attention. The two great armies met face to face in 605 on the banks of the Euphrates at Carchemish and the Egyptian army was annihilated. Although the Pharaoh escaped back to Egypt there was no longer any question of the Egyptians holding on to Palestine. Once more Judah changed hands and Jehoiakim hurriedly shifted his allegiance to the new power of Babylon. Jeremiah saw his chance again. Perhaps the people could be brought to their senses while they were still shaken by this new shock. Jeremiah himself had been forbidden to enter the Temple, so he could not repeat his warnings in person, but what he had said he could write, and a close friend

[1] Jer. 7,4,21–3.

was prepared to take the risk of reading it in the Temple, Jeremiah dictated his prophecies to Baruch and Baruch went off and read them to the people. This time they had a calmer hearing, and the king's council, in session in the palace next door, fetched Baruch into their presence and listened quietly while he read the book to them too. Truly there was a different feeling abroad from that of the impetuous and murderous mob of three years earlier. But it was the same king, and the council must have known in their hearts that he had not changed. Bravely, they carried the scroll in to the king, but they sent Baruch away with the urgent message that both he and Jeremiah must go into hiding. It was a wise precaution, for the king left no doubt about his opinion of Jeremiah's warnings:

> And Jehudi read [the scroll] to the king and all the princes who stood beside the king. It was the ninth month, and the king was sitting in the winter house and there was a fire burning in the brazier before him. As Jehudi read three or four columns, the king would cut them off with a penknife and throw them into the fire in the brazier, until the entire scroll was consumed in the fire that was in the brazier.[1]

Some of the princes were brave enough to protest, but the king's only comment was to send men to arrest Jeremiah and Baruch. Fortunately they

[1] Jer. 36.21–3.

had got away in time, and Jeremiah's first act was to dictate again the words the king had burned.

Jeremiah had already seen clearly that the nation's religion was superficial and corrupt. Now he also saw that the long line of Davidic kings who had governed Judah had also ended in failure. Jehoiakim had thrown in his lot with Babylon, but it would do little to help in the end. Jeremiah must have realized that this king was no more capable of remaining loyal to Babylon than to Yahweh his God. He would rebel and Babylon would inevitably lose patience with the nation and then her judgement would arrive. The Davidic king could no longer be Yahweh's servant; God had given power over his people to the King of Babylon. In a terrible passage Jeremiah showed what his rule would be

> Thus says the Lord of hosts: Because you have not obeyed my words, behold, I will send for all the tribes of the north, and for Nebuchadrezzar the king of Babylon, my servant, and I will bring them against this land and its inhabitants; . . . I will utterly destroy them, and make them a horror, a hissing and an everlasting reproach. Moreover, I will banish from them the voice of mirth and the voice of gladness, the voice of the bridegroom and the voice of the bride, the grinding of the millstones and the light of the lamp.[1]

[1] Jer. 25.8–10.

There is nothing more terrible than this deliberate reversing by Jeremiah of the message of deep joy and laughter which was at the heart of the Deuteronomic hope.

To emphasize his warning and drive it deep into the memories of the people, Jeremiah acted a parable through the streets of Jerusalem. He purchased a large earthenware vessel from one of the potters, and together with some of the leading sympathetic priests and laymen carried it through the streets collecting a crowd as he went. Soon most of Jerusalem was following them. They passed right through the city and out of the gate into the Valley of the Sons of Hinnom south of the city wall. There Jeremiah shattered the pot before the eyes of the crowd, and in the silence which followed explained his action:

> Thus says the Lord of hosts: So will I break this people and this city, as one breaks a potter's vessel, so that it can never be mended. Men shall bury in Topheth because there will be no place else to bury. Thus will I do to this place, says the Lord, and to its inhabitants, making this city like Topheth.[1]

Topheth is the other name for the Valley of the Sons of Hinnom, and a name with terrible associations. Here stood the shrine of Molech where the children were burned alive to Molech well within living memory. It was the first place Josiah had

[1] Jer. 19.9–12.

destroyed and defiled in his cleansing of the land. The people had thrown away their last chance, said Jeremiah, and had shown that they must go the same way as Topheth:

Cut off your hair and cast it away;
　　raise a lamentation on the bare heights,
For the Lord has rejected and forsaken
　　the generation of his wrath.[1]

Sure enough, Jehoiakim's loyalty to his new masters the Babylonians only lasted three years; then he rebelled. At first Nebuchadrezzar was too much occupied with other parts of his new and vast empire to give him his personal attention, and it was not until 598, three or four years after the rebellion, that a Babylonian army marched on Jerusalem. Ironically, Jehoiakim died before he felt the strength of Babylon's power, and his son Jehoiachin (whose other name was Coniah) was left to face a full-scale Babylonian siege of Jerusalem at the age of eighteen. He lasted three months as king, and then the city fell to the Babylonian army. The prophecy of the broken pot had been fulfilled, at least in part, and the people must face their responsibility. They had failed to listen to their God, and the long years of God's patience had ended:

Is this man Coniah a despised, broken pot,
　　a vessel no one cares for?

[1] Jer. 7.29.

6

> Why are he and his children hurled and cast
> into a land which they do not know?
> O land, land, land,
> hear the word of the Lord!

> Write this man down as childless,
> a man who shall not succeed in his days;
> For none of his offspring shall succeed in sitting
> on the throne of David,
> and ruling again in Judah.[1]

Into exile with the king went all the statesmen and the nobles, the skilled workmen, soldiers and priests. But it was nothing like as bad as they must indeed have feared. The king was imprisoned, but it was not a harsh imprisonment, and he was supported from the royal table. Various Babylonian documents have been discovered and deciphered listing the value of the provisions sent to Jehoiachin from the royal household. It appears that the young deposed king was even able to keep some kind of court in his exile. For the rest, they were free to live their own lives and practice their own trades in Babylon. So free in fact, as we shall see shortly, that they thought their exile only a temporary measure and their return to Jerusalem something to be expected at any time.

For the Babylonians did not destroy the city in 698. Far from it. With the leaders safely in Babylon Nebuchadrezzar felt that he need not

[1] Jer. 22.28–30.

even take the precaution of making Judah a Babylonian province. He put a younger son of Josiah, Zedekiah, on the throne, reduced Judah's territory a little, and then withdrew again. It was almost too good to be true, and it is with a sense of almost inevitable disaster that one watches Judah misinterpret Nebuchadrezzar's leniency. It did not occur to either king or people that the Babylonian leniency stemmed from the strength of their position, not from weakness. But it occurred to Jeremiah. Echoing his earlier warning to Jehoiakim, Jeremiah warned Zedekiah in turn to submit to the Babylonian rule and take no liberties with it. Making himself a yoke, the wooden bar which fits across the shoulders to take the weight of buckets, Jeremiah appeared before the king wearing it:

Thus says the Lord of hosts, the God of Israel: I have given all these lands into the hand of Nebuchadrezzar, the king of Babylon, my servant. . . . If any nation or kingdom will not serve this Nebuchadrezzar king of Babylon, and put his neck under the yoke of the king of Babylon, I will punish that nation with the sword, with famine, and with pestilence, says the Lord, until I have consumed it by his hand[1]

But there were other prophets who had the king's ear, and one of them snatched the yoke from

[1] Jer. 27.6,8.

Jeremiah's shoulders and broke it across his knee, saying that God would break the Babylonian yoke within two years. This is what the people wanted to hear, and it is just this kind of false hope which Jeremiah knew to be most dangerous. Not only was it untrue, but it was exactly the teaching to encourage yet another rebellion and finally exhaust the Babylonian patience with this foolish and puffed-up little kingdom. He attempted to undo the false teaching in an equally dramatic way by replacing the light wooden yoke with a cruelly heavy iron one, for it was clear to him that to provoke Babylon could only result in the deepening of suffering. The nation should accept its position of political subjugation and use the opportunity to grow in spiritual freedom by returning to their God. The stirrings of false hopes had even reached the Jews exiled in Babylon, and two prophets in particular were preaching a quick return. To the people in exile Jeremiah wrote a famous letter telling them to settle down and make Babylon their home, for there was no future for them in Jerusalem:

> Build houses and live in them; plant gardens and eat their produce. Take wives and have sons and daughters; take wives for your sons and give your daughters in marriage, that they may bear sons and daughters.... Seek the welfare of the city where I have sent you into

exile, and pray to the Lord on its behalf, for in its welfare you will find your welfare.[1]

And now there began to emerge another Jeremiah—or rather a Jeremiah who had lain buried beneath the weight of the doom he had seen hanging over the people. The picture was becoming clear to him; God's plan for his people was unfolding before him and at last he could see the full pattern. This was not the end of the nation; this was not the end of God's chosen. The false prophets were half right, there was going to be a return. But it must be a changed people who return, a people who had been broken and made again, a people who through suffering had been shown how greatly they needed, and depended on, their God. The change comes in the middle of the letter to the Jews in exile, the nation's leaders:

Thus says the Lord: . . . I will fulfill to you my promise and bring you back to this place. For I know the plans I have for you, says the Lord, plans for welfare and not for evil, to give you a future and a hope. Then you will call upon me and come and pray to me, and I will hear you. You will seek me and find me; when you seek me with all your heart, I will be found by you, says the Lord, and I will restore your fortunes and gather you from all the nations and all the places where I have driven you,

[1] Jer. 29.5–7.

says the Lord, and I will bring you back to the place from which I sent you into exile.[1]

Once sounded this note of hope was never far from Jeremiah. As his personal fortunes declined and his persecution and suffering deepened, so he spoke more and more of the glorious future God was preparing for his people. God was going to rebuild the nation around Jerusalem in holiness and purity and deep joy. But equally certainly the immediate future, said Jeremiah, lay not in Jerusalem but in Babylon.

For all too surely the inevitable happened and Zedekiah, weak and easily led, decided to revolt against the mild Babylonian rule. Just how it happened is not known, but it is very likely that Zedekiah allowed himself to get involved in some scheme which depended on the Egyptians marching to Judah's aid. In the ninth year of Zedekiah's reign the Babylonian army moved swiftly into Judah and after the rapid fall of the outlying fortresses settled down to the long siege of Jerusalem; it was to be more than two terrible years before the city was finally taken. Yet to this period just before the siege began, and to the years of the city's agony, belong the most sublime and tender of Jeremiah's writings. Indeed it is not that he was untouched by the suffering; if anything he was involved in it more than anyone. Because of his open sympathy for Babylon and his re-

[1] Jer. 29.10–14.

peated urging that the city surrender Jeremiah was quickly imprisoned and at one stage, late in the siege, left to die. Only the devotion of a palace servant saved him. But his feet were firmly placed on the solid rock of his sure confidence in the deep and tender love Yahweh has for his people:

A voice is heard in Ramah,
  lamentation and bitter weeping,
Rachel is weeping for her children;
  she refuses to be comforted for her children,
  because they are not.
Keep your voice from weeping and your eyes
    from tears;
  for your work shall be rewarded, says the
    Lord,
  and they shall come back from the land of
    the enemy.
There is hope for your future, says the Lord,
  and your children shall come back to their
    own country.[1]

That hope was sure, and the future was sure, because it did not depend on anything man might try to do; it would not be man's achievement but God's. Too long the people had struggled with a human nature inadequate for the task, too weak for the temptations with which they had been faced. God was going to change all that. No longer would the people try to obey a law imposed on

[1] Jer. 31.15ff.

them from without; God would write his law, the pattern of a holy life, on the very hearts of the people. Their obedience would be spontaneous, a willing obedience springing from their innermost being, flowing from a new covenant in which the people themselves would be renewed:

> Behold, the days are coming, says the Lord, when I will make a new covenant with the house of Israel and the house of Judah. . . . I will put my law within them, and I will write it upon their hearts; and I will be their God, and they shall be my people. And no longer shall each man teach his neighbour and each his brother, saying, know the Lord, for they shall all know me, from the least of them to the greatest, says the Lord; and I will forgive their iniquity, and I will remember their sin no more.[1]

Here is the truth which the Deuteronomist dimly glimpsed; here is the true source of man's salvation and the only way it can be achieved. At the moment when the old Hebrew history ended and the long glory of the Davidic kingdom was finally eclipsed, Jeremiah looked back over that history and his people's failure and saw the truth written clearly in it. It is too hard for man to climb to God, he is too tightly bound. Man's salvation must be God's work; it is too hard for man. External

[1] Jer. 31.31,33f.

law, even law which has had breathed into it the inspiration of the vision of God, is not enough. An enforced reform, even when it is imposed with the highest motives, is bound to fail. Josiah's attempt to impose Deuteronomy on his people had proved that. God himself must work in the hearts of his people, taking and blessing and remaking them. Only then will his people know the radiant joy of spontaneous response to God, the full satisfaction of life filled with his goodness:

> He who scattered Israel will gather him,
>> and will keep him as a shepherd keeps his flock.
> For the Lord has ransomed Jacob,
>> and has redeemed him from hands too strong for him.
> They shall come and sing aloud on the height of Zion,
>> and they shall be radiant over the goodness of the Lord . . .
> Their life shall be like a watered garden,
>> and they shall languish no more.
> Then shall the maidens rejoice in the dance,
>> and the young men and the old shall be merry.
> I will turn their mourning into joy,
>> I will comfort them and give them gladness for sorrow.
> I will feast the soul of the priests with abundance,

and my people shall be satisfied with my
goodness, says the Lord.[1]

There is little more to tell, and what little there
is only serves to bring into sharper contrast this
most remarkable of men who saw so deeply and
clearly into the heart of God and, in the midst
of desolation, spoke of what he had seen.

Towards the end of the siege the king had
Jeremiah fetched to him secretly, so that his
council should not know, and he asked him what
he should do. Surrender, said Jeremiah, and the
Babylonian will still spare your life and the city.
"I am afraid of the Jews who have deserted to
the Babylonians," said the king, "lest I be handed
over to them and they abuse me." Nothing Jeremiah could say would convince him. They parted
again, Jeremiah back to prison, the king back to
his hostile council. The end came quickly. The
wall was breached and the king captured while
trying to escape. Nebuchadrezzar beheaded his
two young sons before his eyes and then had him
blinded so that it should be the last thing he
remembered seeing. Jerusalem was reduced to
the ground and the survivors driven in gangs to
slavery in Babylon.

Only the very poorest of the peasants remained,
under the control of a Hebrew administrator,
Gedaliah, appointed by the Babylonians. Jeremiah chose to stay with him. Mizpeh, just a little

[1] Jer. 31.10–14.

north of Jerusalem, was chosen as the administrative centre, for Jerusalem had been so completely destroyed that it was uninhabitable. But even this last pathetic remnant of government was not to last. Three months later a gang of Jews who had escaped deportation by fleeing to the desert arrived in Mizpeh and were entertained hospitably by Gedaliah. As they were all eating at his table they suddenly rose and murdered him, and then killed seventy out of eighty pilgrims from the north who were unfortunate enough to arrive at that moment on their way to Jerusalem. Such responsible Hebrews as were left pursued the murderers, but they escaped across the Jordan into Amman. Their pursuers were left in a terrible dilemma. Certainly Babylon would avenge the murder of its governor and they would have great difficulty proving that they themselves were not the guilty ones. In their despair they decided to flee to Egypt forcing Jeremiah to go with them, and in Egypt we lose sight of him.

He has no need of our pity, nor of the pity so many scholars have spent on him. For all his suffering he was not always a sad man. By the end of his life he had travelled a long way from the anger and bitterness of his youth when he first tasted opposition. Throughout his life God watched and protected and directed him, and towards the end gave him an insight into his character deeper than any who had gone before him.

> Before I formed you in the womb I knew you,
> and before you were born I consecrated you;
> I appointed you a prophet to the nations. . . .
> Be not afraid of them,
> for I am with you to deliver you, says the
> Lord.[1]

This was true; and not only of Jeremiah, but of his nation as well.

NOTES

Historical Background

Main sources:
2 Kings (4 Kings) 22–25.30
Jer. 40–44.30

Kings of Judah:

638–609: Josiah

609: Jehoahaz. Josiah's son; reigned three months; taken prisoner to Egypt by Pharaoh Neco

609–598: Jehoiakim. Josiah's son; died naturally; other name was Eliakim

598: Jehoiachin. Jehoiakim's son; reigned three months; taken prisoner to Babylon by Nebuchadrezzar. His other names are Coniah and Jeconiah

[1] Jer. 1.5,8.

598–586: Zedekiah. Josiah's son; blinded and taken
          prisoner to Babylon by Nebuchadrezzar.
          His other name was Mattaniah

Governor of Judah:

586: Gedaliah. Murdered after a few months

Other kings:

Assyria:	668–625:	Ashurbanipal
Babylon:	625–605:	Nabopolassar
	605–561:	Nebuchadrezzar
Egypt:	609–593:	Neco
	593–588:	Psammetichus II
	588–568:	Apries

Main events:

621: Reform based on Deuteronomy
612: Babylonians capture Nineveh, capital of
      Assyria
609: Josiah killed at battle of Megiddo
606: Last of Assyria
605: Egyptian army defeated by Babylonians
598: First siege of Jerusalem by Babylonians
589–587: Second Babylonian siege of Jerusalem,
          city destroyed.
586:      Gedaliah murdered; Jeremiah taken to
          Egypt

The text of Jeremiah shows signs of much revision
and rearranging. The first book dictated by Jeremiah
to Baruch was destroyed by King Jehoiakim (see
Jer. 36.21–3), and although Jeremiah then dictated
another one he may not have given his prophecies in

the order in which they occurred. At least four hundred years later the book still had not reached the form in which we now know it, and was still being rearranged by editors.

1	His call
1.11–12,13–16	The two visions
11.18–23; 12.1–17	Persecution:
20.1–13; 26.8–24; 32.2–5; 37.11–15; 38.1–13	By family and neighbours
4.5–8,11–21,23–8, 29–31; 5.15–17; 6.1–5,22–6, and perhaps 6.5–21	The Scythian threat
2 and 3	Religious situation before Josiah's reform
11.1–8	Jeremiah's support of the reform
7.1–16; 26.1–6	Condemnation of Temple complacency
14.13–18; 23.9–40; 27.9–22; 29	Condemnation of false prophets
7.5–7; 20.12; 22.3,13–19	Social justice
	Symbolic actions:
13.1–11	The spoiled loincloth
19.1–12	The earthenware pot
27.1–11; 28.1–17	Yokes
31.31–4	The New Covenant
30.1–3,16–22; 31	Hope, joy and restoration
29	Letter to the exiles in Babylon

8

CONCLUSION

W<small>E</small> have reached the end of our study and now we must try to gather up some of the fragments. At this moment more than any other we should do well to remind ourselves again of the principles and limitations we have accepted. You and I cannot help but be people of our own time and place—twentieth-century Western Christendom; but at least we can beware of judging these people whom we have been studying by our own times and our own standards. We must try to do some summing up, but we must try to do it still through their eyes and by their standards. We may indeed find that their standards and the things they took for granted in their lives are preferable, even, to our own; be that as it may, at any rate we can at least try not to prejudge them, and we can try to use our own experience only so far as it illuminates and enlightens theirs. In our world it is increasingly difficult to avoid committing your loyalty to either the Communist Powers on the one hand, or the Western Powers on the other. This should at least help us to appreciate the ancient Hebrew dilemma of choosing between alliances with Egypt or with Babylon. We too live in a capitalist society where comfort and security and a higher income are incentives motivating people. This too will help us to understand what was going on in the heart of an ancient Hebrew merchant or a workman building village houses or a farmer anxiously wondering what he could do to make sure that his crop would not be a failure, and will help us to see the temptations to which they were exposed. They are not temptations which lie entirely outside our own experience.

It is towards the end of the year 586. The Babylonian army has been gone for perhaps a year, taking with them all the citizens of Jerusalem and everyone of any consequence or with any skill throughout the country. The ruins of Jerusalem have settled and the fires died out. Weeds have begun to spring in the streets and the shells of the houses, hiding the debris of pieces of clothing and personal odds and ends which were too mean to attract looters. The Temple and the royal palace next door to it have both been levelled to the ground. Only the very poorest peasants have been allowed to remain in the country. There is not much stock left after a large Babylonian army living off the land for two years, but what there is the people who remain are free to take. From time to time they need to hide from small bands of plundering Hebrews who have fled into the desert, and there are Babylonian army patrols on the move watching for any signs of an Egyptian attempt to march north again. We have seen something of the events which have led up to this during the previous 170 years and of the people who have taken part in them. Are there any outstanding features in the pattern of those years?

One of the most noticeable features is the urgent need for social reform. For this we have the evidence of every one of the major prophets of those years; each of them insisted that abuses of the Law and corruption in the courts and wrongful claims of privilege and wealth must all be stamped out if the people were to be loyal to God and were to claim his protection. He was a God who cared about the way people treated each other; if his people did not give to each his due and respect each man his neighbour, whether he were poor or rich, city-dweller or country peasant, then God would make his power known. His care for them was not unconditional; he required that they accept his standards and put them into practice in their lives—both their domestic lives and their public and business lives. Perhaps they exaggerated, those prophets, but there can be no doubt about their concern, nor the absolute standard they brought to bear on their people. Amos's plumbline is not his own private

7

opinion of what is upright, it is God's; and the lack of the knowledge of God, said Hosea, is the cause of the corruption:

> There is . . . no knowledge of God in the land; there is nought but swearing, lying, killing, stealing, and committing adultery; they break all bounds and murder follows murder.[1]

Isaiah blamed the leaders of the community, the elders who had the responsibility and who should have been the guardians of justice and the protectors of the weak, and, taking up and developing a theme which had already found mention in Amos and Hosea, he attacked the nation's religious life.

The religious life of the nation, the inconsistency between the social life of the people and their religious practices, is the second obvious feature in the pattern of this period. There seemed no suspicion in people's minds that it might be hypocritical to worship when the worshipper is not accepting the standards of the God whom he worships:

> What to me is the multitude of your sacrifices? says the Lord;
> I have had enough of burnt offerings of rams and the fat of fed beasts; I do not delight in the blood of bulls, or of lambs or of he-goats.

[1] Hos. 4.1–2.

When you come to appear before me, who
requires of you this trampling of my courts?
When you spread forth your hands I will hide
my eyes from you; even when you make many
prayers, I will not listen; your hands are full
of blood.
Wash yourselves; make yourselves clean; remove the evil of your doings from before my
eyes; cease to do evil, learn to do good; seek
justice, correct oppression; defend the fatherless, plead for the widow.[1]

There are similar passages in Amos, Hosea and
Jeremiah. The main point is obvious. Mere conformity to the external forms of worship is useless;
more than that, it is blasphemy. Worship is giving
God his due, acknowledging his worth, and this
can only be done by obeying his will and respect-
ing his desires and trying to become as like him
as is possible for a man. The worshipper is
enacting a lie if he does not take his God's
standards into his life; he is publicly acknowledging his God's worth and privately denying it. At
best this reduces religion to superstition: actions
without meaning performed in the hope that they
will bring prosperity. It is not far removed from
magic.

So much is clear in the prophetic teaching, but
we must be careful that we do not thereby con-

[1] Isa. 1.11–12,15–17.

clude that the prophets of this period condemned the sacrificial system itself, that they tried to remove the sacrifices from Hebrew worship. This was far from their intention. Their concern was to see that the sacrificial worship expressed the truth at the heart of their religion: that God had delivered the nation and had made them his own people, that he wanted for them the true satisfaction of all their hopes in communion with himself and that their sacrifices should be their way of expressing their utter dependence on him. The sacrifices were never intended as a way of pacifying an angry God, or satisfying his tyranny with an unfortunate victim's death, or even as a way of diverting his attention from the worshipper's misdeeds—a sort of bribe to encourage the judge to turn a blind eye. This indeed they were if the worshipper went on in his own way refusing to allow the character of his God to make any difference to his life. Then men might well ask what kind of God such a man thought he was worshipping, and what he thought he was up to with his sacrifices, what he thought he was doing. No, the sacrifices were the method God had given his people that the communion, the intercourse, the familiarity between them, broken by his people's disobedience, might be restored again. The essential heart of the sacrifice, the reason for it, was not the pacifying of God; this is why the word "propitiate" is so misleading and a wrong translation of the Hebrew. The sacrifice was for the worshippers' benefit, the way by which he could share in the innocent and pure life of the sanctified victim, and so himself receive something of that innocence and purity and sanctity and with it be able to stand before his God again. The Hebrew word *kaphar* means "to cleanse". It is something God does for the worshipper, not something the worshipper does for God. What the prophets saw so clearly and stated so strongly was that it is sacrilege for the worshipper to take advantage of that cleansing, to enter into God's purity and sanctity, and at the same time make no effort to turn away from the deeds which have defiled him, which have put him in need of cleansing:

> I will not listen; your hands are full of blood.
> Wash yourselves; make yourselves clean; remove the evil of your doings from before my eyes.[1]

So much for sacrifices to Yahweh, their own God, the God of the Hebrew people. Sacrifices to any other god were an entirely different matter, but for the same basic reason: the character of those gods. No other god demanded righteousness of his worshippers because no other god was himself righteous. The intercourse between priest and priestess or worshipper and sacred prostitute which lay at the centre of the fertility cults was

[1] Isa. 1.15f.

little better than magic; it enacted the intercourse between the god and goddess, the Baal and his Astoreth, which was thought to bring fertility to the fields and stocks. There is no thought here that the god *cares* for the people; their fortune is no more than an accidental by-product of his pleasure. It is unlikely that the worshipper of such a god will care any more than his god for the people around him; and the worship itself, by its promiscuity, breaks down the very heart of the family and the forces of mutual trust which hold it together. There is no possible connection between such a system and morality. Nor indeed is there when the worshipper believes that his god will only smile on him through the smoke of burning children. With such sacrifices and such gods there can be no compromise.

The Prophets were only trying to draw out the implications of the great saving acts by which, in the nation's history, their God had shown himself to them and let his people know what he required of them. They were only applying the tradition Moses had founded to their own times and their own problems, as Moses had pointed to the apparently impossible series of events by which they had got away safely from Egypt, and had seen in them the assurance that their God cared for them, so, too, the prophets pointed back to those same saving acts as the sure proof that God was concerned still. At first they could

draw no other conclusion than that his concern
for his people must now mean their punishment.
He had placed his honour in their keeping and
they had defiled it with their spiritual disloyalty
and their spiritual corruption; they must be
destroyed. Only by absolute punishment could
God's absolute righteousness be protected.

This statement is a little extreme even for
Amos, but his vision of the plumbline set in the
midst of the people, and their punishment for any
deviation from it, is not far removed. It was
Hosea who saw the inadequacy of this view.
From the heart of his own misery and longing for
his unfaithful wife, he saw that the love he still
had for her must be a pale reflection of the love
God still has for his people even when they betray
him. Punishment there must be, but it must be
remedial punishment, purging which can restore.
But Hosea was still thinking in terms of the
nation as a whole, that corporate unity which
is never far from Hebrew thinking. It is with
Isaiah that the true beginning of personal responsibility begins. He built on all who had gone
before him; their teaching that God is indeed
concerned for his people found its fulfilment in
his vision of God enthroned in majesty in the
Temple in the midst of Jerusalem. But he was
no longer hopeful that the whole nation could
survive. Perhaps his failure to turn the king away
from the fateful appeal for Assyrian help was

the moment of truth for him. He realized that without royal support and leadership the nation as a whole could not be moved, and at the same time saw that this did not mean the destruction of everyone. All would suffer in the general chaos which Isaiah, with his clear penetration into the political realities of his time, saw must inevitably come; but those individuals who remained faithful would emerge as a remnant, a holy people, ready to lead the nations to God.

The Prophets did not receive royal support, or if they did at all, it was only for the time of some passing crisis, some sudden emergency, and there was neither the consistency nor the whole-heartedness which alone could give their teaching power over the people. Then as now, the little man, the man with a small business or a plot of land or a reasonably secure job, wanted to keep his peace and security more than anything else. He wanted freedom from worry and a chance to support his wife and bring up his children and keep in with his neighbours. If the king or the local big landowner or even the elders of his village wanted things the way they were he was not going to make a fuss about it. Certainly he was not going to jeopardize his own position. Trouble enough came along in the normal way of things without going and looking for it. If the wife went off to the local shrine of Astarte up the hill who was he to stop her? Everybody else's wife was there, including the elders' wives, so there couldn't be too much wrong with it. And if he went off with the other men to the Baal shrine in the wood outside the village who could blame him? He wasn't being unfaithful to his wife in any way different from the rest of his friends, and in any case this was a religion, not adultery, and a man dare not take any risk with his crop. He made the proper sacrifices to Yahweh as well, three times a year, and told the children the story of the Passover and how their great-great-grandfathers had escaped from Egypt. No-one could say he was being unfaithful to Yahweh. No, the prophets would not find many listeners amongst the ordinary people, or if they did there were too many forces working against them for their teaching to be remembered for long.

But one group, or perhaps even only one man, remembered and looked forward to a time when a king would put all his authority and power behind the Prophets' teachings, and with the guidance and support of the priests, cleanse the land and force the people to conform to the pure vision of God first given to Moses and explored ever deeper by the prophets. The Book of Deuteronomy is his memorial, the blueprint for the reform he probably never lived to see. For it was not until a full seventy years after Isaiah that all the essential conditions occurred to make the reform a practical possibility. The stifling control

of Assyria was weakened as troops from her outlying provinces were drawn into the death-
struggle with the Babylonians. A young and
enthusiastic king in Jerusalem was ready to take
the plunge and purge his kingdom of the imposed
Assyrian religion and every other spiritual influence which might lead men away from Yahweh
their God. All the old familiar laws, the accumulated customs and precedents of more than six
hundred years, which the anonymous lawyer had
collected and codified, were enforced. They had
been so arranged and edited and combined with
an explanatory framework and commentary that
they could be a vessel for the distilled essence of
the Prophets' teaching, and for the Mosaic tradition about God and his great saving acts and his
love for his people and his steadfast faithfulness
to his promise for them. By a ruthless destruction
of all that opposed or hindered it, and by an iron
control of all religion by the Jerusalem priests, the
Law was imposed on the people. This is the key
moment in the nation's history, the crisis, the
turning-point, the check in the flight from God.
But all too soon it became clear that it was no
more than a temporary halting. With the young
king's death in a wasted gesture defying overwhelming Egyptian power, the nation drifted
back to its old ways. The moment had passed, the
crisis was over and the reform had failed.

It is doubtful whether the reform could ever

really have succeeded. Perhaps if the king had lived long enough to control a whole new generation it would have taken root. But it is at least questionable whether reform could be achieved by these means, by royal commissioners with soldiers at their backs, leaving behind them not only desecrated pagan shrines and, in some cases, slaughtered pagan priests, but also ruined village shrines dedicated to Yahweh their own God and a local priesthood humiliated before their people and denied their age-long right to sacrifice in their own villages. A great queen nearer our own times, caught in the turmoil of religious change imposed by force, said, "I will not make windows to look into men's souls." She recognized clearly that outward conformity to the official religion was as much as she could hope for. Perhaps Josiah came to realize this in time, but whether he did or not, his reform certainly failed to change the hearts of his people. And Jeremiah quickly recognized it.

It is Jeremiah's tragedy that he has gone down to history as a prophet of doom, a sad man. He has added a word to the English language. "A Jeremiad", says the dictionary, "A lamentation, a doleful complaint." But there was nothing *essentially* doleful about him. It was his misfortune to live at a time when his people's blindness and stubbornness and complacency and treason were going to bring upon them inevitable catastrophe, and it was his misfortune to be able to see further and more clearly into the situation than anyone else. Only three years after the reforming king's death there came, close on the heels of fleeing Egyptians they had just defeated, the new power of Babylon; a power more patient and lenient and enlightened in its control of the territories conquered than Assyria had been, but still not a power of inexhaustible patience. It was Jeremiah who saw that religious faithfulness is infinitely more important than political freedom, and who saw, moreover, that Babylonian government, unlike that of the earlier Assyrians, would not interfere with the religion of their subject peoples. But his insight was lost or ignored in the shifting politics and fears of palace manœuvring and intrigue.

Yet even at the blackest moments Jeremiah did not forget that these were still the Chosen People of God and that God was going to keep to his choice. Rather, as the final destruction of Jerusalem became clear to all within the city, Jeremiah saw through the present disaster and suffering into a future when these people would have learned their lesson and would accept their God on his own terms. Then, when they at last trusted him and his way with them, his presence amongst them would be the centre of the world's hope and his people's glory. From the ruin and horror of a city in the last stages of a siege it is understandable that Jeremiah should write:

Thus says the Lord,
I have dealt you the blow of an enemy,
   the punishment of a merciless foe,
Why do you cry out over your hurt?
Because your guilt is great,
   because your sins are flagrant,
   I have done these things to you.[1]

Yet at the same time he could also write:

I have loved you with an everlasting love;
   therefore I have continued my faithfulness
      to you.
Again I shall build you, and you shall be built,
   O virgin Israel.[2]

And both are true. But it is no small gift to have
the insight to see it and the courage to say it, and
it is indeed a remarkable vision which at this
stage in her history foresaw the nation not only
restored to God's favour, but restored in her
original purity, restored in her virginity. It takes
one's breath away that a man can write like this
knowing the corruption of the previous two
hundred years. Yet is is true, for fundamentally it
is an insight into the heart not of the people but
of God. The restoration will be God's work, how
can it be less than complete? The restoration will
be an act of re-creation by the God who made the

[1] Jer. 30.14.
[2] Jer. 31.34.

heaven and the earth and who keeps all things and all peoples in their ordered place in his plan; it will be *complete* re-creation.

All this is clear to Jeremiah, but what of the people who had carried their chains to Babylon, how did they view it? At first, as we might expect, with great bitterness, and not only against Babylon but more especially against their old neighbours in Palestine who had assisted the Babylonians and had delighted in the destruction of Jerusalem. In almost every detail, with one very important qualification, the destruction of the northern kingdom of Israel was repeated in the southern kingdom of Judah 135 years later. Then Judah had rejoiced at the fall of Samaria, now in turn her own neighbours watched gladly as Jerusalem fell. The people's bitterness is preserved in one of the psalms:

Remember, O Lord, against the Edomites
    the day of Jerusalem,
How they said, Raze it, raze it!
    down to its foundations!
O daughter of Babylon, devastator!
Happy shall he be who requites you
    with what you have done to us!
Happy shall be he who takes your little ones
    and dashes them against the rock![1]

[1] Ps. 137.7–9.

It is ironical that Judah, once so much a daughter of Assyria, now in her time of reckoning turned on Edom for being daughter of Babylon.

We must resist the temptation to follow the exiles too far into Babylon, or in too much detail, for the more one looks into their life during those years the more fascinating it becomes and the more impressive their achievement. They were not without guidance. From the beginning Ezekiel was one of the exiles; having been taken to Babylon with the first select groups in 598 he did much to guide his countrymen to the full significance of the events. He was at one with Jeremiah, who was in Jerusalem at the same time, in doing all he could to discourage the exiles from expecting a swift return to Jerusalem. But more than this Ezekiel picked up and developed two of the great themes which the Prophets who came before him had tried to teach the people: the presence of God with his people, and God's faithful mercy and steadfast love towards them.

The Prophets' task was to make the people realize not only what their God was like and what he required of them in their daily lives, they were equally concerned to teach that he was with his people and active amongst them. And not only with the Hebrews; he also used the great colonialist powers as his tools, the instruments with which he controlled and directed his world. But while the nation was firmly in possession of

its own land it was difficult to move away from
the idea that God's authority and power was
confined to that area. At best he could only be
seen, at any rate by the ordinary people, as the
chief God, the most powerful God, overruling
when necessary, the power and authority of other
gods, but not the *only* God. Ezekiel, like Isaiah
and Jeremiah before him, had much to say of the
majesty and glory of God, but a God present with
him and the other exiles in Babylon. Like Isaiah,
he had a vision of God present and active amongst
his people, but whereas Isaiah's vision was set in
Jerusalem's Temple, Ezekiel's visions were on the
banks of a river in the heart of Babylon. For the
first time there could now be effective condemnation of foreign gods and idols, not because they
have no place amongst Hebrews, but because they
have no truth in them. The way was cleared for
the realization that God intended to restore not
only his own special chosen people, but all people
and that the vocation of the Hebrews was to be
the centre to which all people could come to worship the Hebrew God, the only God.

But like Jeremiah, Ezekiel saw that there had
to be radical change in the people before this
vocation could become practical, and this change
was beyond the people's own ability. It had to be
God's work, God's creative work, and moreover
it must issue solely from his innermost being, not
from any merit the people could claim. For if they

stood before their God and asked for strict justice, asked for their rights, they could only expect condemnation. God would perform this restoration to demonstrate to all the world that he *is* God and is not going to allow himself to be humiliated by the misery his own chosen people have brought upon themselves, and by their faithlessness:

> Thus says the Lord God: it is not for your sake, O house of Israel, that I am about to act, but for the sake of my holy name, which you have profaned among the nations to which you came. And I will vindicate the holiness of my great name.... For I will take you from the nations, and gather you from all the countries, and bring you into your own land. I will sprinkle clean water upon you and you will be clean from all your uncleannesses.... A new heart I will give you, and a new spirit I will put within you.... I will put my spirit within you, and cause you to walk in my statutes and be careful to observe my ordinances.[1]

Towards the end of the exile period, not fifty years after the first Hebrews had been carried to Babylon, and not forty years after the destruction of Jerusalem, a prophet emerged whose name we do not know, but whose writings are the high-water-mark of the ancient Hebrew penetration into the character of their God. His teaching is to be found

[1] Ezek. 36.22,24–7.

in chs. 40 onwards of Isaiah. His realization of
God's ever-present powers controlling and directing the world he alone has made and which he
alone sustains was the consummation of all previous Hebrew experience. But more than that,
in four poems which have been named the Songs
of the Servant he reached through to an insight
unlike anything else in the Old Testament:

> Behold my servant, whom I uphold, my chosen
>   in whom my soul delights;
> I have put my spirit upon him, he will bring
>   forth Justice to the nations.[1]

Who the prophet meant by the "servant" is not
absolutely clear—perhaps some unknown martyr
in Babylon, perhaps even Jeremiah, but there is a
strong possibility that he was referring to the
nation as a whole, Israel the beloved of Yahweh:

> And he said to me, You are my servant,
>   Israel, in whom I will be glorified.[2]

So he wrote in one of the poems. But it is what the
servant has done that is important:

> Surely he has borne our griefs
>   and carried our sorrows;
>   yet we esteemed him stricken,
>   smitten by God and afflicted.

[1] Isa. 42.1.
[2] Isa. 49.3.

> But he was wounded for our transgressions,
>> he was bruised for our iniquities;
>> upon him was the chastisement that made us
>>> whole,
>> and with his stripes we are healed.[1]

It is that insight I should like to leave the reader
with: the unknown anonymous prophet of Israel
looking dispassionately at his people's catastrophe
and seeing there more than well-deserved punishment for past unfaithfulness. He saw his nation
as the chosen of God and the centre of his design
for bringing salvation to the world, but they now
stood at that centre because in some sense they
had carried the weight of the world's unfaithfulness:

> All we like sheep have gone astray;
>> we have turned every one to his own way;
>> and the Lord has laid on him the iniquity of
>>> us all.[2]

> It is too light a thing that you should be my
>> servant
>> to raise up the tribes of Jacob
>> and to restore the preserved of Israel;
> I will give you as a light to the nations,
>> that my salvation may reach to the end of the
>>> earth.[3]

[1] Isa. 53.4–5.
[2] Isa. 53.6.
[3] Isa. 49.6.

BOOK LIST

It is not easy to know what to suggest from the enormous number of books available on the Old Testament, but the following will certainly be found useful:

GROLLENBURG, L. H., *Atlas of the Bible*. This contains, in addition to the excellent maps, a large commentary on the history and a lot of photographs. There is also an abridged edition. (Nelson, 1956)

DE VAUX, *Ancient Israel, its Life and Institutions*. The best general study of the whole life of ancient Israel. (Darton, Longman & Todd, 1961)

HEATON, E. W., *Everyday Life in Old Testament Times*. (Batsford, 1957)

BOUYER, C., *The Meaning of Sacred Scripture*. (Darton, Longman and Todd, 1961)

CHARLIER, D., *The Christian Approach to the Bible*. (Sands, 1958)

ROWLEY, H. H., *The Faith of Israel*. (S.C.M., 1956)

HEBERT, A. G., *The Throne of David*. (Faber, 1941)

The information on these maps has been intentionally kept to the minimum, since their purpose is simply to give the reader a clear indication of the geographical background to the history, and especially to the relationship between Israel and her neighbours. There are many good biblical atlases available today to which the reader may refer for more detailed information—for example *The Westminster Historical Atlas of the Bible*, ed. G. E. Wright and F. V. Filson, London, S.C.M. Press; L. H. Grollenberg, *Atlas of the Bible*, trans. and ed. H. H. Rowley and Joyce M. H. Reid, London and Edinburgh, Nelson; *Oxford Bible Atlas*, ed. H. G. May, R. W. Hamilton and G. N. S. Hunt, O.U.P.

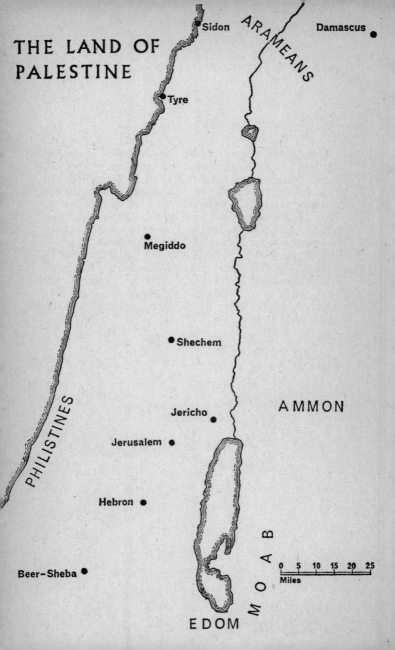

INDEX OF NAMES AND SUBJECTS

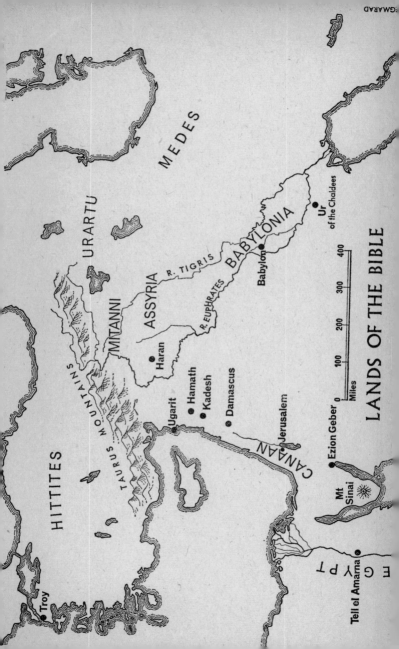

LANDS OF THE BIBLE

INDEX OF BIBLICAL REFERENCES